Just One Of The Many –
A Navigator's Memoirs

Dudley Egles, 1943

Just One Of The Many –
A Navigator's Memoirs

Dudley 'Pop' Egles

(ex 148, 462, 614 Squadrons R.A.F.)

The Pentland Press Limited
Edinburgh • Cambridge • Durham • USA

© Dudley C. Egles 1996

First published in 1996 by
The Pentland Press Ltd.
1 Hutton Close
South Church
Bishop Auckland
Durham

British Library Cataloguing in Publication Data.
A catalogue record for this book is available
from the British Library.

ISBN 1 85821 401 7

Typeset by CBS, Felixstowe, Suffolk
Printed and bound by Antony Rowe Ltd., Chippenham

This book is dedicated to my dear wife, Eileen, without whose persistent encouragement it would never have been written.

CONTENTS

FOREWORD

BY WING COMMANDER T.W.H. HEWER, CD, psac, pfac
Royal Canadian Air Force, Ret'd.

'ENGLAND EXPECTS THAT EVERY MAN WILL DO HIS DUTY'

When Nelson made that now-famous signal to the British fleet at Trafalgar, he must have done so with much confidence. In fact his exhortation was met with some mystification. Admiral Collingwood was heard to grumble, 'What is Nelson signalling about? We all know what we have to do.' Some seamen complained, 'We've always done our duty.'

Those reactions reflect the fact that for centuries the soldiers, sailors and latterly airmen of those sceptred isles have ever gone 'once more into the breach', often poorly led, always in discomfort and danger. This memoir is written by one of those airmen in World War II who shrugged off their fears, their hurts and their losses, and 'got on with the job' – who did their duty.

The author takes the reader on quite an extensive tour of the western hemisphere as he trains, instructs and navigates his crews to enemy targets in North Africa and Europe. Along the way he becomes a member of every unofficial 'club' established by those who fly, including: the Goldfish Club, for those whose lives were saved at sea by the use of a dinghy; the Late Arrivals Club, whose badge is the flying boot with wing, open only to those returning from behind enemy lines and avoiding capture; and the Caterpillar Club, for those who saved their life by use of a parachute. A charmed life?

The reader is given an intimate look into the basics of Royal Air Force aircrew training, and into the mysteries and tools of air navigation. The perils and rigours of flying over and operating from the fiery cauldron of the Egyptian Western Desert, where summer temperatures often exceeded 130° (F) come graphically to light. Some of the tactics of that élite group of squadrons, the Pathfinder Force (PFF) are revealed. These were the most experienced and skilled airmen who flew in the van of the main bomber force to find and place visual markers on the target. This often involved very low flying at night under poor weather conditions, or a long, steady run-up to the target which gave the anti-aircraft defences extra time to bring their guns to bear on the Lancaster, Halifax or Mosquito bombers of the day. It was a hazardous operation on the best of nights.

As one follows the author's postings, from basic and operational training, from squadron to squadron, in convoy at sea, from continent to continent, one may reflect on the continual, massive movement of personnel and material throughout the whole period of the war. The magnitude of the support structure required to place the fighting troops, properly trained and equipped, in the line against the enemy, stretches the imagination.

The author's matter-of-fact and sometimes whimsical style belies the stresses and strains of operational flying on Bomber Command, especially on one who flew two tours of operations, and served in other capacities for almost the whole of the war, ending up in a prisoner-of-war camp. The reader will discern his courage and the skill he acquired as a navigator. The pilot captain of the crew was, of course, all-important, but the navigator was the key the crew relied upon to locate the target, get the bombs away and get them home safely to base. Dudley's delightful descriptions of some of the lighter moments between engagements with the enemy and even in the midst of some of the sorry plights in which he and his crew found themselves, give testimony to the youthful humour they were able to dig down and find to sustain them.

It may be useful and establish some authority for these words if I recount briefly how I come to be writing them. Like most Canadian aircrew members of the R.C.A.F. who arrived in England in 1941 or early 1942, I was posted to an R.A.F. squadron. Thus I had the privilege and the challenge of flying alongside the Dudley Egles of the R.A.F. I first met Dudley in December, 1941 on 148 Squadron, based at Kabrit, Egypt. In March, 1942, Dudley's crew was one of two who did not return from one of our many raids on the port of Benghazi, Libya, the storied 'mail run'. About a week later, as I walked from my tent towards the sergeants' mess, I came face to face with Dudley and three other members of his crew. They had just arrived back at camp from their escape across the desert. I pulled out my ever-present camera, and they posed for me. Standing there, with an assortment of broken ribs, a broken nose and ankle, and numerous bruises, they managed a smile.

Fifty years later, in May 1993, I flew to England for a 148 Squadron reunion, and there I shook Dudley's hand again. Not surprisingly, he did not remember me taking that photo which had lain in my wartime album all those years. Before I left Dudley gave me a copy of the manuscript for his book and honoured me greatly by asking me to write a few words of introduction to it. I am sure some of my words will embarrass this modest man and I am aware that I cannot do justice to his story.

The reader will decide whether the author extended service to King and Country to its limits, and whether, in spite of his chosen title, *Just One of the Many*, he did in fact belong to an élite few. No matter, he relied on his comrades in arms as much as they relied on him, often for life itself. Surely, Shakespeare's Henry V would say of those men, as he did of his own men before Agincourt,

'We few, we happy few, we band of brothers'.

Howard Hewer

Chapter 1

EARLY LIFE

I was born in Pulborough, in Sussex, on my father's sixtieth birthday, when my mother was forty-three, and I was taken to Bognor at the age of four days. My father, who died when I was fourteen, was both an apprenticed baker and pastrycook and an apprenticed painter and decorator, and was able to follow either of these crafts. I attended Lyon Street School, Bognor, and won a scholarship for Chichester High School at the age of eleven, but at this time my family moved to Hove, and so I attended Varndean School for Boys in Brighton up to the age of seventeen, having taken the School Certificate. I started working for local government in Brighton Corporation Electricity Undertaking. My hobbies were swimming and cycling. My friends and I swam almost daily in the sea off the pier, summer and winter, and we cycled everywhere. When I met Vicky, who later became my wife, she was living in Romford, Essex, and I cycled there most weekends to see her, a round trip of about 120 miles.

Early in 1939, shortly after my eighteenth birthday, I tried to join the R.A.F., but my mother would not sign the form of consent, so I applied to join the Volunteer Reserve and was accepted for Aircrew training but there was a waiting list for pilot training of at least a year; the waiting list for Observers was shorter, so I signed on as an Observer. Nothing happened; I did no training, but was told that if there was an emergency I would be called up immediately.

On September 1st, 1939, the V.R. were called up, and I attended the R.A.F.V.R. H.Q. in Hove, joined a long queue of other hopefuls, and eventually reached the desk, manned by an R.A.F. corporal, who asked me my number. The only number I had was 3, (3 on the waiting list), so I told him that my number was 3, and he told me to 'p*** off', as nobody had a number like that. I told him that was the only number I had but he said that he could only take those with official service numbers, so would I please go away, or words to that effect.

After some fuss I managed to see an officer who told me that he was unable to do anything for me and suggested that I apply to the local recruiting office 'in the usual way'. I did this, my particulars were taken and I was assured that I would be called up 'well before Christmas'. I continued to pester the recruiting staff almost daily, but Christmas came and went and the Royal Air Force managed to struggle on without me.

Chapter 2

BASIC TRAINING

Eventually in April 1940 I received a letter requesting my presence at R.A.F. Uxbridge for three days. I put on my best suit, packed a change of shirts and underwear, pyjamas and three handkerchiefs, borrowed two pounds from my mother and set off. On arrival at Uxbridge I was given the statutory 'intelligence' tests, a full medical and an interviewing board at which I was told that I was 'fit Aircrew' and asked what I wanted to be. I naturally opted for pilot training and was informed that there would be a waiting list of a least a year. I was, of course, somewhat shattered by this pronouncement and I pointed out rather strongly that I had already been waiting over a year. This unfortunately was to no avail.

I went then to the N.A.A.F.I. for a drink to try and drown my sorrows. I must have looked very miserable indeed for I was approached by the ubiquitous Corporal with the words, 'Wad's matter, lad?' I explained my predicament and he informed me that he was in the recruiting section and knew a way out of my trouble. It appeared that the R.A.F. were accepting those who wished to train as Observers, who did exactly the same basic training as pilots and then it would be 'a piece of cake' to re-muster as pilot. I was a little dubious about this but the Corporal took me to see a Flight Lieutenant who confirmed the, to me, good news. The next day I 'joined' as a u/t Observer. I expected to go home for a while but was told I was now 923039 A.C.2 Egles D.C. and would start training immediately. I was issued with uniform and shown how to mark everything with my number, how to make up a bed 'in an airmanlike manner', given some very basic foot-drill and physical jerks and a few days later posted to R.A.F. Manston, Kent, where we did nothing but foot-drill, rifle drill and P.E. for a month. We were still hoping to see an aeroplane - that's what we had joined for! When the course at Manston had finished four of us were posted to R.A.F. Bircham Newton in Norfolk to do 'ground defence'.

Chapter 3

GROUND DEFENCE

On our arrival at R.A.F. Bircham Newton, which was an operational station with Swordfish aircraft, we were greeted by the Station Warrant Officer who informed us that we looked a reasonably smart bunch and should know our foot-drill so we were to report to Station Sick Quarters at 1600 to act as pall-bearers. This we did and were told that the deceased was a pilot who had been killed in action and we were to convey the coffin to the local railway station for onward transfer to his family. With great dignity we slow-marched the coffin to a truck and took it to the railway station, accompanied by a Corporal. We were shown the railway carriage which was to receive our burden and prepared to carry at slow march, only to be told by the Corporal, 'Don't worry with all that bull, it's mostly rocks in there anyway! Bung it in and let's get back!' So much for the dignity of death.

The next day we were detailed for what our American friends call K.P. – Kitchen Patrol. We were issued with potato peelers – the hand variety – and a veritable mountain of potatoes with instructions to 'Get that lot peeled then!' This was a fairly soul-destroying task and seemed to have little connection with ground defence, although we supposed that an Air Force, like an Army, marched on its stomach.

Fairly early the next morning, while we were still helping to feed the station personnel, an L.A.C. (Leading Aircraftman) wandered in and asked if any of us could drive. I had been warned, of course, against volunteering for anything, but had had enough of potato-peeling to last me a life-time, so I immediately said that I could drive. In fact I could only drive a motor cycle, but what sort of vehicle had not been specified. 'Right,' said the L.A.C. 'You're now my mate. I'm a lorry driver and the S.W.O. (Station Warrant Officer) has a job for us.' Outside the kitchen was the vehicle - an enormous truck with an equally enormous trailer. I told the L.A.C. that I had never driven anything so big - how true! - but he said that didn't matter, he would be doing the driving, it was just 'regulations' that he had to have a mate.

We duly reported to the S.W.O. who reminded us that there was a war on and that R.A.F. Bircham Newton would need to be defended if the expected German invasion took place, so we were to proceed with all haste to an M.U. (Maintenance Unit) near Carlisle to collect barbed wire to help with the aforesaid defence. We were not, to use his actual words, to stop for a 'shit, shave or shower!' We then set off on our journey across the breadth of England, arriving at the M.U. in the very early hours of the morning. We managed to wake a rather irascible stores Flight Sergeant who informed us that the barbed wire we were seeking was still at the railway goods yard. Remembering the instructions of our S.W.O. we duly went to the goods yard, only to be told that the person who could give us permission to collect the barbed wire would not be on duty until 07.00 hours. We managed to scrounge a cup of tea and some biscuits from the railwayman and went to sleep in the cab of the lorry.

At 07.00 the man with the permission arrived and said, 'That's the truck over there. Help yourselves!' On asking for help in loading our vehicles we were met with a blank refusal. So, still remembering the S.W.O.'s orders, we started our mammoth task. After some little time getting scratched, we managed to borrow some industrial gloves from the railway people, which protected our hands somewhat, but did not save our uniforms. These were the days before battledress, when our 'best blue' was also our 'working blue'. Somehow we completed our loading, and after snatching a cup of tea and some sandwiches from the railway canteen, we set off on our return journey.

It was now dark again. After a few hours the driver said that he had to rest and that I would have to take over the driving. I reminded him that I had never driven a vehicle of such size, but he persuaded me that it was 'a piece of cake'. Somehow I managed to get the mammoth moving – fortunately there was virtually no traffic – and the driver almost immediately fell asleep. All went well for an hour or so until we were descending a long gradient. I was by then feeling quite confident in my driving ability, until the trailer started swaying a little. I yelled for help to the driver but he was dead to the world. I really was frightened, until we reached the bottom of the descent and the road started climbing quite quickly. With the aid of good old Sir Isaac Newton and his gravity I was able to bring the vehicle to a halt. I sat shaking like the proverbial leaf until I could wake the professional driver. He had slept all through my period of terror. We completed our journey back to our unit with no further mishaps.

On our reporting to the S.W.O. he noted the very dilapidated state of our uniforms and gave us chits to draw new ones from the stores and packed us off to bed. He did NOT ask us to unload our vehicle. The next day I noticed that the barbed wire was piled near the stores. Over two years later, I happened to visit Bircham Newton and saw that barbed wire was still piled near the stores. I cannot swear that it was the same barbed wire, but I have my own thoughts!

The next day I was able to join my three original companions and we were told to report to the armoury. Ground defence at last, we thought. On arrival at the armoury we were met by, of course, a corporal. I'm sure the R.A.F. could not function without corporals. He introduced us to a fearsome piece of weaponry. 'This is the Vickers watercooled machine gun.' It was the gun we had all seen in many films. 'You have to know how to strip it,' he continued and proceeded with the dexterity and speed of a stage magician to reduce the weapon to its component pieces. We were absolutely bewildered.

'Well, I suppose I'd better show you once more,' he went on and reassembled and dismantled the gun again at incredible speed. 'Now you've seen how to do it twice, so I want you to do it. I'll be back in half an hour.'

There we were, left with these unfamiliar pieces of metal. What a problem. We were supposed to have a reasonably high standard of intelligence so we attacked our task with some determination, and I shall never know how, but in some lucky fashion we managed to reassemble the Vickers watercooled just before the return of the armourer corporal. We were pleased to note that he was somewhat surprised at our result. We were then taken to the range, shown how to load and fire the gun and clear simple stoppages, issued with a thousand rounds of ammunition and told to enjoy ourselves on the firing range. This we did with much gusto - after all, we really were only overgrown schoolboys.

The following day we were instructed to report to the control tower with the Vickers plus ammunition and given a sandbagged position on the highest point. We were told that two of us had to be on duty at all times and we were to arrange our own shifts.

This seemed to be a good arrangement to us and it lasted for two and a half days. We were then posted to Hastings to I.T.W. (Initial Training Wing.) We could now put up the white flash on our caps which signified 'aircrew in training'.

Chapter 4

I.T.W.

On arrival at Hastings we were put in an hotel almost opposite the pier. This apparently was a condemned building, but was considered good enough to sleep aircrew under training. In the whole edifice there was only one serviceable toilet, this to be used only in the direst emergency. To offset this problem we were each issued with a card with the R.A.F. crest on one side and the Hastings Coat of Arms on the other, together with the legend 'Admit bearer free of charge to Public Convenience opposite Hastings pier'. We had often heard that in the Service one needed a chit to do virtually anything, but this seemed to be the absolute limit. Our aircrew training started in earnest with lectures on navigation, theory of flight, Morse code, etcetera, together with foot drill, rifle drill and P.T.

After some weeks we were all moved to Torquay and again billeted in hotels. Mine fortunately had serviceable plumbing, but my 'room' which I shared with a six-foot-four companion had literally been a linen cupboard. By some strange coincidence, about fifteen hundred girls employed by the Prudential Insurance Company were also billeted in Torquay at the same time, or was this some superb planning by the powers that were? On our first visit to the local pubs we found that in the majority of them only cider was sold. We bitter drinkers from the south-east expressed disapproval – cider was no drink for men! This was before we had been persuaded to try some 'rough'. At fourpence (just under 2p. for those of you who don't remember pre-decimal coinage) for a pint it needed very little expenditure to obtain a nice alcoholic glow. This facility, plus the also lonely Pru girls and the better billets made Torquay seem not at all a bad place to be.

We were divided into flights, each under a Senior N.C.O. and a corporal. I was in C Flight of No. 3 Squadron of 5.I.T.W. Our S.N.C.O. was Flight Sergeant Monks and our Corporal's name was Lumrod. The Flight Sergeant who was grey haired and wore First World War medal ribbons seemed quite ancient to us. There was a current popular film about the R.A.F. called *The Lion has Wings* and almost daily the Flight Sergeant (we dared not call him merely ' Flight'!) greeted us with the cry, 'Maybe the lion has wings but Flight Sergeant Monks has claws!' Corporal Lumrod was a most interesting character. He was Norwegian, spoke at least five languages, had represented Norway in the Olympics, was a classical violinist of very high calibre, owned a Rolls-Royce (the Squadron Commander had a bicycle!) and was one of the nicest chaps I have ever come across. He took us for foot and rifle drill and, of course, P.T. He was extremely strong. I then weighed around thirteen stone, and he could lift me off the ground with one outstretched arm grasping my collar. He was quite wealthy and was most generous to us two-shillings a day peasants. (Ten pence in modern money).

One morning Corporal Lumrod announced, 'Tonight ve haf a party, because in ten days my vife vill be coming.' His English accent was apparently the worst part of his linguistic ability. Those of us who availed ourselves of his invitation were plied with cider in a room he had hired in a local pub. Three days later we were told 'Tonight ve haf a party. My vife comes in seven days!' and the generosity was repeated. Finally the announcement came, 'Tonight ve haf a BIG party. My vife comes tomorrow!' This indeed was a memorable thrash. We played a strange, apparently Scandinavian game. Two fellows stood at opposite ends of a longish dining table, cried 'Skol', downed a pint, crawled under the table to the respective other ends where a further pint awaited each of them; they repeated the process until one called quits. There were very soon 'bodies everywhere'. We heard some months later that Corporal Lumrod had been commissioned into the Intelligence Branch. I wondered how they got on with our Norwegian friend.

Our I.T.W. course eventually finished and I found that there were about thirty of us who had joined as u/t (under training) Observers hoping to remuster as u/t Pilots. For some reason I was chosen to approach the C.O. with our problem. The C.O. told me that the medical standard for pilots had been raised somewhat since we had joined. After some discussion the C.O. said that he would arrange a further medical for us. This took place and a few chaps were failed. The remainder were told that we were now u/t Pilots. Great joy!

Chapter 5

NAVIGATION SCHOOL

Two days later we were told that we were posted to Navigation School in Canada. So much for my Pilot training. We drew tropical kit to use as summer uniform in Canada and went by train to Gourock near Glasgow to board the liner, *Cape Town Castle*. Funny, we thought, but that is where we disembarked – Cape Town! The vessel had not been converted to a troopship and we still had stewards to wait upon us. By now we had all been promoted to L.A.C. (Leading Aircraftsman) which gave us no disciplinary powers but a vast increase in daily pay, from two shillings (ten pence) a day to five shillings (twenty-five pence). The price of whisky on board was four pence, old money. On the second day out we saw a four-engined aircraft approaching. 'Ah, obviously a Sunderland – good old Coastal Command!' we agreed. A few minutes later we were machine-gunned by the plane. It was, of course, a Focke Wolfe Condor. So much for our hours of aircraft recognition study.

Apart from our small group of u/t aircrew the rest of the passengers on board were army personnel en route to Singapore or the Middle East. For some reason they did not seem to be good sailors on the whole and when we hit rough weather the cases of *mal de mer* were legion. I have fortunately never suffered from either seasickness or air sickness, but I well remember one

No. 1 course, Empire Air Training Scheme, Oudtshoorn, South Africa. 1940-41. D. Egles, back row, 2nd from left.

occasion when I nearly succumbed. I had picked my way through various green-complexioned soldiery to go down to the mess deck for lunch, only to discover that the dish being served was tripe. It was not my choice of food at any time, but the sight of it under those circumstances was almost too much for my stomach. I made my way to an open deck and fresh air at great speed.

We landed eventually at Cape Town and were put on a train to Oudtshoorn in Cape Province. This used to be the centre of the ostrich feather industry in South Africa in the days when the wearing of such plumage was considered by the ladies to be *de rigueur*. One ostrich farm, as far as I remember, was still functioning. On arrival in town we were met by the Mayor and Town Band, and entertained to a dance in the evening. All very pleasant. We discovered that we were No.1 Course of the Empire Air Training Scheme in South Africa. We had Anson aircraft and pilots, but no navigation equipment, parachutes or harnesses. These had apparently been lost in transit – some efficient U-boat commander, no doubt. We learned our navigation with the aid of foot-long wooden rulers, semi-circular protractors and very crude pairs of compasses, but we *did* learn how to navigate. We also learned how to retract the Anson undercarriage manually (was it 125 turns?) and how to make an ostrich egg omelette. All you need is a hammer and a ginormous frying pan. I seem to remember that one ostrich egg is equivalent to two dozen hens' eggs.

Our course passed all too quickly. Hard and interesting work interspersed with visits to the coast at Mossel Bay where the South Africans entertained us very well indeed. There was of course no blackout and no rationing. A superb mixed grill cost the equivalent of less than ten new pence. Oudtshoorn itself had a cinema, called a bioscope, where we, (the whole course) actually saw *Gone with the Wind*, and went across to the local hotel bar for refreshment during the interval. We found the South Africans very friendly on the whole but we did have some trouble with the O.B., (the Osseva Brandwag - I think that's how it is spelt) - the Boer anti-British movement. There were odd fights and we were not allowed to go out of camp in less than twos.

At the end of the course, which we all passed, we were sent to Cape Town to board a boat for England where we would do our Bombing and Gunnery courses. On arrival at Cape Town we boarded a ship (for the life of me I cannot remember the name of it), learned that we had the rest of the day free and were to report back on board at 23.50 hours. Three of us, (Gordon Georgeson, another whose name escapes me, and I) set about exploring the city and met a member of our course, Jim Wright, who was convalescing there after suffering a broken skull. He introduced us by telephone to three sisters, all under twenty, who lived on a vineyard at Wynberg; they insisted on coming in to town and driving us about to see the sights. We all ended up in a nightclub, which I believe was called the Blue Moon, where we danced and drank until the girls drove us back to the docks at about 01.20 hours. We found our vessel (I must have known the name of it then!) and went on board, only to find our cabin empty and no signs of any R.A.F. personnel. We found a crew member who informed us that the remainder of our party had disembarked just after midnight, but he had no idea where they had gone. We decide to spend the rest of the night on board in our cabin.

At approximately 07.00, Gordon and I decided to go on deck for some fresh air. We met one of the ship's officers who wanted to know what R.A.F. bods were doing on his ship. He told us that they were weighing anchor in half an hour so we had better make ourselves scarce. This we did, but we had great difficulty getting *out* of the docks. After achieving this we found, after many inquiries, that there was an R.A.F. liaison officer in a nearby building known as the Castle. With some trepidation we approached this gentleman, to be torn off a lengthy strip, and told that our homeward voyage had been postponed – 'exigencies of the Service' – and that the rest of our course had been sent to a S.A.A.F. camp on the outskirts of the city. The Flight Lieutenant informed us that as there was no transport available we would have to go by bus, and that we would then be confined to camp as a punishment for our absence. He then seemed to relax a little and said how relieved he was that we had turned up as he had not relished having to explain to those higher up the loss of three airmen. He asked if we had money for the bus fare, and gave us money from his own pocket for that and also sufficient to buy breakfast.

On arrival at the camp we found that our fellow course members were just considering sharing out our kit. We spent five days confined to camp and then the Flight Lieutenant visited us and cancelled our punishment. We quickly contacted the sisters and were invited to meet their parents on their grape farm, where we were entertained royally. The South African people were as usual most generous. Life was very pleasant indeed for the next few days until we once again embarked for England.

Chapter 6

BOMBING & GUNNERY & O.T.U.

We landed at Liverpool and entrained for London and R.A.F. Uxbridge. When it was found out that we had completed our Navigation training we were told that we were now sergeants and sent to the stores to draw the necessary tapes to embellish our uniforms. The next day we were posted to West Freugh in Scotland to do our Bombing and Gunnery courses, which would complete our full Observer training. We arrived and were met by the Station Warrant Officer who appeared dumbfounded on seeing us resplendent in pristine stripes. He said that he had expected a course of L.A.C.'s (Leading Aircraftsmen) but would we come into the Sergeants' Mess and have a drink! Up until then an S.W.O had always been a sort of archangel and completely unapproachable. To be offered a drink by such a being was completely beyond our expectations. He than explained that he had no suitable quarters available for Senior N.C.O.s and would we please use airmen's billets until he could arrange the correct accommodation for us.

All went well until the next evening when we were told that the promotion to S.N.C.O. rank was premature and we were to revert to L.A.C. This was a little disappointing but most of us had not expected promotion until the end of the B.& G. course.

The next day our problems started. We were virtually

persecuted by S.P.s (Service Policemen). We were all wearing shoes, which was permitted wear for those who had been wearing tropical kit. We were continually stopped with the cry 'Airman!' The following dialogue then ensued.

'Yes, corporal.'

'You are wearing shoes!'

'Yes, corporal.'

'Airmen wear boots!'

'But I've just come from South Africa.'

'Take them off and let me see the Air Ministry Stamp.'

'Yes, corporal.'

'Now put them back on.'

The regulations decreed that, although we were quite often flying again within the hour, we must change from flying kit to ordinary uniform to go to the Mess, (a rule more honoured in the breach than the observance in normal circumstances). Our billet was only a few yards from the Airmen's Mess and there was an S.P. permanently waiting to see if any of us was 'improperly dressed' and to order us to change if not. It turned out that two of our course had foolishly torn strips off a Corporal S.P. on the first day there when we thought we were sergeants. *No-one* tears strips off S.P.s and gets away with it . . .

One morning we were having lectures on ballistics and were given a ten-minute N.A.A.F.I. break. The N.A.A.F.I. canteen was very close to the classroom and we trooped in for the usual 'cuppa'. I happened to be last in line and the 'pot' became empty just before I was served. A fresh brew quickly appeared but it was literally boiling when served to me. (It's supposed to be, isn't it?) By the time I had quaffed sufficient to alleviate my thirst I was alone and fearful of being late back to class. From the door of the canteen was a well-worn though unofficial path across the grass back to the lecture rooms. I was half-way across this path when I heard the dreaded cry 'Airman!' An S.P. was calling to me in his usual dulcet tones.

'Yes, corporal.'

'You're walking on the grass!' (Apparently a heinous crime.)

'No, corporal, there's no grass here!'

'If I say you're walking on the grass, you're walking on the grass. You're on a charge!'

For that misdemeanour I was awarded seven days 'jankers' for 'walking on the grass whilst on active service'.

Our first visit to the Parachute section caused no little consternation. We were issued with harnesses and parachutes but of course we did not know what to do with them. We had never seen such equipment before and the Sergeant in charge took some convincing that we had flown some fifty hours without their use.

The aircraft we flew here were Fairey Battles, with Polish pilots who were excellent 'drivers airframe' but most had an extremely limited command of English. On one occasion I had finished my gunnery detail - we used V.G.O. (Vickers Gas Operated) machine guns against drogues - (a drogue is a canvas cylinder, not unlike a windsock, towed behind another aircraft) - and my pilot turned to me and gave me a thumbs-up signal. I assumed that he meant that we had finished and would be returning to base. But no! The plane's nose went down very sharply as we screamed toward terra firma; the pilot pulled out (just in time, it seemed to me), climbed very steeply indeed and looped! I had never experienced this manoeuvre before and I was clinging on for dear life. When we landed the pilot explained to me, in very broken English that he was not sure that a Battle was fully aerobatic and wished to find out!

We were allowed most Saturday afternoons and Sundays off, so each weekend three of us, Clarkson, Georgeson and I used to go to Portpatrick, about ten miles away, have several jugs of ale in the local on the Saturday evening, stay the night, and work off our hangovers by battling our way round the golf course on the Sunday. We had one number three iron between us so the standard of play was not of the highest calibre by any means, but we enjoyed it immensely and it was a sanity-saving break from the rather arduous time we were experiencing at West Freugh.

The course was completed and we could now legally put up our 'tapes' again and we were awarded our Observer brevets. We now really were Sergeants and members of the 'Airborne Orifice' Club, so called because the 'O' for Observer was the shape of an orifice, or hole. This, of course, had a less polite nomenclature used by other aircrew 'trades'.

Our posting was to R.A.F. Harwell in Oxfordshire, an O.T.U. (Operational Training Unit) which had Wellington Mark 1 aircraft – twin-engined bombers. Here we met pilots, wireless operators and airgunners and formed ourselves into crews. The Wellington was familiarly called a 'Wimpy', after a character in 'Popeye' called 'J. Wellington Wimpy'. The standard Wimpy crew at that time was two pilots, observer, wireless operator, front gunner and rear gunner. The observer was navigator, bomb-aimer and spare airgunner. At the age of nineteen I was the oldest member of my very first crew and was immediately nicknamed 'Pop' which stuck throughout my R.A.F. service. Not long afterwards, our crews were rearranged and a new rear gunner joined us. His name was Tony and although he was an 'old man' of thirty, I still kept my nickname, 'Pop'.

We started night-flying in earnest and completing longer and longer flying exercises. Towards the end of our course we took part in 'nickel' raids – dropping leaflets over Paris and bombing various airfields on the Continent. I remember being shot at by

Bombing and Gunnery Course at West Freugh, Scotland 1940.
D. Egles, back row, second from left.

light flak on crossing the French coast on the way to bomb an airfield near Amiens and then on our return trip being on the receiving end of quite a heavy A.A. barrage on crossing the English coast – in spite of I.F.F. – Identification Friend or Foe, an automatic radar transponder giving a coded reply if friendly – which was fitted to our aircraft. Fortunately no damage was done, except perhaps to our nerves.

Chapter 7

FIRST TOUR

On completion of our course we were posted to 148 Squadron which was at that time based on Malta, and equipped with Wellingtons (Wimpies).

As some aircraft had apparently been shot down flying to Malta via Gibraltar at night, we were detailed to fly out in daylight. This was mid-1941 and Malta was under siege. We were laden with spare barrels for Bofors light anti-aircraft guns, which were being used up at a rate of knots in defence of the beleaguered island.

Our trip from Hampstead Norris, a satellite 'drome of Harwell, was fairly straightforward, until we landed at Gib. These were the days before the runway was extended into the sea. All we had to land on was the old racecourse, which did not give us much room to spare. When we went for debriefing we were immediately asked two questions. 'Why was your I.F.F. (Identification Friend or Foe) switched off?' and 'Why did you allow your trailing aerial to wrap itself round the mast of a ship in the harbour?' We had, of course, not switched off the I.F.F. and on getting the ground staff to check it, they found that the Graviner switch had somehow triggered and destroyed the I.F.F. The Graviner switch was a self-destruct mechanism on the I.F.F. to prevent the I.F.F. getting into enemy hands. The trailing aerial problem was pure finger trouble. The Wireless Operator had simply forgotten to reel it in. We *were* a little tired after eleven hours in the air!

We had a meal, re-fuelled, installed a new I.F.F. and went to a dreamless sleep, at least it was so for me. The next morning we took off for Malta. The actual take-off was pretty dicey as the runway on Gib. was extremely short and we were heavily laden with gun barrels and full fuel tanks. The end of the runway was where the sea started and we seemed to dip almost into it as we left terra firma. We had been warned that the Luftwaffe was very active on Pantellaria which was not far off our course, so were told to fly at 'deck level' in the hope of avoiding enemy fighters. I well remember that we were very close behind the aircraft flown by Peter Mayhew of our squadron and I was watching him from our astro-dome. Peter had taken the 'deck level' orders very much to heart and literally bounced his rear turret on the briny several times. I mentioned this to his rear gunner after we had landed at Malta. Bert Field the 'bounced' gunner was a true blue Cockney, and his description of the episode had to be heard to be believed. I thought that I knew all the expletives, but obviously I didn't.

We spent a short time on Malta and then our Squadron, 148, was posted to Egypt. We delivered our aircraft as instructed to Abu Sueir, an M.U. (Maintenance Unit) not far from the Suez Canal. There we were given a meal and when we asked for a billet were told to pick any tent near the Sergeants' Mess. We did this, but on wandering round a little we found some spare S.N.C.O's hutted quarters so we moved our kit to the more amenable billet. That night the Luftwaffe decided to raid Abu Sueir and we found, on examination the next morning, that the tent we had originally picked had been destroyed in the air raid. What a fortuitous move!

The crew were then posted to join the squadron at Kabrit, an

Home! 148 Squadron. R.A.F., Kabrit on the Great Bitter Lake, Egypt 1942. (Photo by H. Hewer)

airfield on the Great Bitter Lake, south of the Suez Canal. Life there was mostly lived in tents, at least for S.N.C.O. aircrew. Even our mess was a tent and each crew was housed in a E.P.I.P. (Egypt pattern, India pattern) tent, which was dug into the sand.

As observer, I had to cope with an entirely different form of navigation in the desert. These were the days before Gee (a ground-based navigational aid) or H2S (an airborne navigational radar) and the only radio beam we could get was from Malta, which was quite difficult to receive and would only give one position line anyway. Visual navigation, (map-reading) was quite unlike that in Europe. There are no towns, rivers, lakes or railways to be seen in the desert - except over the Nile delta. You will probably ask, what about astro-navigation? That is really not accurate enough. Navigation came down to D.R. (Dead Reckoning) and finding the angle of drift, (the angle between the course steered and the actual track made good over the terrain). At night this was done by throwing out a four pound incendiary bomb - a supply of which was kept beside the flare chute - and the rear gunner sighting his guns on the resulting fire and reading off the angle of drift on a graticule attached to his turret.

Operational aircrew were given four days leave every month or so, and the usual place to go was Cairo where there were shops, restaurants, night-clubs and cinemas. On our first leave as a crew we booked into a pension in Cairo, had a meal and the next day went to the main cinema which had *air-conditioning*! We were about half-way through the programme when I developed an excruciating pain in my stomach. It became so bad that my knees were as close to my chest as I could get them. I really was in agony. My crew called the S.P.s (Service Police) who organised an ambulance which took me to hospital. I

looked up from my stretcher as I was taken into the building to
read with horror the words 'Maternity Ward'. We had always
been told that the Air Force could do anything to you except
make you pregnant. Was I the exception to the rule? However it
turned out that I had malaria and dysentery, which I suppose is
better than male pregnancy. I spent a rather unpleasant week in
the hospital and then returned to my squadron.

My crew had temporarily taken on another navigator and I
was feeling rather spare in the crew-room when the Squadron
Commander came in, looked at me and asked, 'Are you any
good as a navigator?'

'I'm bloody marvellous, sir,' I replied.

'Good,' he went on, 'you're on ops with me tonight.'

The target was the shipping and harbour of Benghazi -
known as the Milk Run as it was so often attacked by us. We
had to fly from Kabrit to an advanced landing ground in the
desert, land, refuel and then press on. The flight to the target
was uneventful and we bombed it as ordered. We returned to
the L.G. but on E.T.A. (Estimated Time of Arrival) the ground
was blotted out by a sandstorm.

'Are you sure the L.G. is down there, Navigator?' asked the
skipper.

'Oh, yes, sir,' said I. I had worked to the best of my ability
and it should have been there. We lost height preliminary to
landing and as we approached the proposed landing spot we
were able to contact the duty pilot on the TR9, a short range
radio, which confirmed my navigation, and showed that we
were where I had intended. Then the fun started. Only one
wheel of the undercarriage would come down. The pilot climbed
to an altitude sufficient to enable him to dive and pull out
sharply in order to try to shake the offending wheel down, but
to no avail. Then it was discovered that the wheel that had been

'Wimpy' 148 Squadron. R.A.F., circa February 1942 (Photo by Howard Hewer).

lowered successfully would not retract which prevented us doing a belly landing. Landing on one wheel is somewhat more dicey, but the skipper was a very experienced driver and made a beautiful job of it.

Odd incidents which happened on this tour come to mind, and may be of interest to my readers. One of them concerns Dougie, a pilot friend of mine. On his way back from one of the 'milk run' ops. to Benghazi he had to pancake in the desert not too far from the Nile delta. He made a successful belly landing and in no time at all was surrounded by itinerant Arabs.

While waiting for assistance he thought he would amuse them. Dougie was a 'fine figure of a man' – some six feet two and a keen rugger type. He strode in majestically among the Arabs with his arms outstretched in front of him, carrying a red tin. With some ceremony he placed the receptacle on the ground in the midst of his by now interested audience, drew himself up to his full height, opened his flies and directed a stream into the tin. Immediately a great sheet of flame erupted. Consternation from the assembled throng, cries of 'Allah!' and general wonderment and fright. The tin was, of course, a Mark 1 Flame Float which was standard luggage in Wimpies those days. Before appearing before the gathered throng, Dougie had pulled the drawstring of the bag of calcium phosphide in the tin. On contact with water, phosphene is generated which takes fire spontaneously on contact with air. The wonders of modern science.

On one operation we raided some Jerry airfields south of Benghazi and dropped hundreds of Caltrops. The Caltrop was a device rather like two bent double sharp-ended nails welded together. No matter how they fell, at least one point was uppermost. The idea, of course, was to puncture aircraft tyres.

Our base at Kabrit was rather a long way for the enemy to come and we had very few air raids, but two days after our Caltrop dropping exercise a Junkers 88 appeared, in daylight, over our runway and dropped *our* Caltrops back on our airfield.

Chapter 8

COMING OF AGE

My twenty-first birthday was on the 8th February 1942 and on the night of the 7th/8th the Squadron was detailed to attack Piraeus, the port of Athens, and my crew were on the operational list. All went well to the target, which was shipping and fuel storage tanks at the port, and we bombed successfully. Our route home to Kabrit took us over Crete which was by then occupied by the Germans. On approaching the island we could see that it was completely covered by cloud. As my navigation was solely by D.R. (Dead Reckoning) I needed to obtain a drift. Tony, my rear-gunner, felt that the cloud was too thick to be able to see the required incendiary illumination from the incendiary bomb thrown out for this purpose, but we threw one out anyway as we overflew the cloud covered island.

The result was spectacular indeed. We decided later that the bomb must have hit the senior flak (*FliegerAbwehrKanone* – German 'aircraft defence gun') officer on the head, for suddenly the sky was full of bursting shells. Tony made the comment that we could have got out and walked on the flak, but of course we did not. The defence fire was much more dense than it had been over the target and we had dropped only one tiny four pound bomb!

As we left the island Tony was able to get me a drift on a

white building and he informed me that it was at the limit on his graticule of 45 degrees to port. I had never previously experienced such a high drift so I immediately asked the pilot to alter course to compensate, while I rapidly calculated a 'new wind'. We had been really thrown about in the unexpected flak attack over Crete and some shells had burst perilously close to us.

Some little while later I began to feel very uncomfortable in the seat area – a sticky fluid feeling. Oh no! I thought, I can't have! I gingerly felt down the rear of my trousers (quite an acrobatic feat in full flying kit – Irvin suit, Mae West and parachute harness), and in the red light over my navigation table saw my hand covered with an ominous dark fluid. I called the wireless op. to confirm my worst fears and he brought a torch and discovered that after all it was only blood! A stray piece of shrapnel must have penetrated first the aircraft, then my metal chair, then my flying gear and finally come to rest in me. It was not painful, and I felt quite relieved at the reason for my discomfort. We landed safely at base and I was able to change my clothing and relate my coming of age experience to the debriefing officer. What a birthday present! Shot in the bot!

Chapter 9

MUTINY

I had been given a few days leave and decided to go to Tel Aviv by train, a journey of several hours. Once there, I booked into an hotel and deposited all my kit in my room before setting out to visit all the sights in the area. I enjoyed a few days wandering around, and on the last day I asked the desk clerk to arrange a taxi for me early next morning to take me to the station for my return journey to Kabrit. 'I'm very sorry,' he informed me, 'there's no possibility of a taxi tomorrow, as it's Yom Kippur.' That is the Day of Atonement for the Jewish people, a day of fasting and not working. We discussed the alternatives, but the only one was my walking to the station with all my kit. As the station was some distance out of town, that was ruled out.

I decided that I would have to be a day late in returning to base. 'They can't shoot me for it,' I thought. Little did I know! On arrival I signed in at the guardroom, and on my way to my tent I met the Disciplinary Sergeant, who said, 'I see you got back eventually. I hope you haven't signed in yet.' When I told him that I had, he called me a stupid so-and-so, as he could have fixed it for me if I had seen him first. 'Now you'll automatically be on a charge, aircrew late on returning home from leave, and you will have to appear before the Group Captain, the Camp

Commandant.'

The Camp Commandant was very cross, gave me 'a severe reprimand', to be recorded in my personal file, and ordered me to carry my bombsight to the furthest dispersal every morning for a week. This may not sound very arduous, but the bombsight was very heavy, especially in its carrying case, and the furthest dispersal was about a mile away.

I reported my offence and its punishment to the Squadron Commander, Wing Commander Rainsford, who told me that I must accept the Reprimand, but that I could forget about carrying my bombsight to the dispersal point every morning for a week.

At about 11.00 hours one day, after having been on 'ops.' the previous night, I wandered into the Sergeants' Mess to see if anything was happening and I read a notice pinned to one of the tent poles ordering all Senior N.C.O. Aircrew to parade outside the S.W.O.'s (Station Warrant Officer's) office at 13.00 hours. I went back to our crew tent and informed the rest of the chaps. I should point out that N.C.O. aircrew were billeted in tents away from the main camp. The ground crew 'erks' had wooden quarters round the station parade square. My message was received with various impolite remarks, pointing out that we were allowed a day off after flying most of the night on operations. Nevertheless the majority of the bods turned up on parade at the required time. We were met by the Flight Sergeant Discip. who marched us to the armoury, issued us all with rifles, took us to the parade square and informed us that we were going to do rifle drill.

We told him that as S.N.C.O.s we used small arms (we were issued with revolvers) and that we were certainly not going to do rifle drill on our rest day in front of umpteen 'erks' who were sitting outside their billets or taking siestas around the parade square. The Flight Sergeant then marched us back to the armoury where we handed in the rifles, and then back to the S.W.O.'s office.

The S.W.O. himself appeared, took over the parade, marched us back to the armoury, re-issued the rifles, took us back on to the square and informed us that the Station Commander, the Group Captain, had ordered that we S.N.C.O. aircrew were to do rifle drill and that he, the S.W.O., was going to see that we did it. On the Squadron were several Australians and one of them, who shall be nameless, told the S.W.O. in no uncertain antipodean terms into which part of the S.W.O.'s body the rifle should be inserted - not too gently, either!

'That man - report to the Guard Room - under Close Arrest!' Most of us, (unfortunately not all), accompanied our Aussie comrade to the Guard Room and asked to be to be placed under Close Arrest as well. The few (very few) non-criminal types stayed and did their rifle drill. Of course when we arrived at the Guard Room and asked to be put under Close Arrest it was found to be impossible. Kings Regulations stated that a person under Close Arrest must always be escorted by two persons of equal or senior rank, and as we made up the bulk of the Squadron there were nowhere near enough S.N.C.O.s to perform the requisite duty. We were therefore told that we were to consider ourselves under Open Arrest, (which did not entail the escorts).

We went back to our Mess and were met by our Squadron Commander who by now had heard about our 'mutiny'. We pointed out to him that although we were under arrest we naturally did not want to stop flying and he agreed that that would be possible. Life for the majority of us went on as usual, but the main perpetrator, the Aussie, was confined to his tent under escort, awaiting Court Martial. This did not occur for many weeks, during which time he had cleaned out most of his escorts at poker. We were put on charges and were 'severely reprimanded' and denied three months seniority. When the Court Martial took place the Aussie was reduced to the rank of Aircraftsman, sentenced to thirty days 'glasshouse' (military prison), which he did in an Australian establishment, and as a supreme punishment, *sent back to Australia!*

My 'severe reprimand' for the mutiny was duly recorded in my documents along with the previous one for returning a day late from leave, and they remain there to this day.

Reunion of the 'Mutineers', May 1993 at R.A.F. Marham. 'Turkey' Rainsford, C.O., left rear, Howard Hewer, 4th from left, Dudley Egles - right.

Chapter 10

THE DAY WHEN ALMOST EVERYTHING WENT WRONG

At the last count it appeared that I belonged to a dozen clubs connected with the Royal Air Force, and four of them I did not particularly want to join. This is how I happened to join one of them.

In North Africa, Rommel had advanced his Afrika Korps as far as Sollum, having by-passed Tobruk which was still held by the Allies, although it was being besieged by the Afrika Korps. The Libyan port of Benghazi was the sole source of supply for Rommel, and so it was regularly bombed by our bomber squadrons, so regularly that we called it 'the Milk Run'.

Operational aircrew were allowed four days leave a month and my crew and I were due for our four days. We could, and did, therefore, have more than our usual few pints of 'Stella', the local brew, that evening, knowing that we should not be flying next day.

A new crew had joined the squadron and it was customary for the experienced crews to provide a 'screened observer' to accompany the new lot on their first operation; it was the turn of the Navigation Leader, but he suddenly went sick overnight and next morning I was detailed to replace him, although my crew were going on leave. I turned up for briefing with a bit of a hangover, and was given a route from base, (Kabrit) to LG

(Landing Ground) 106, which was just a strip of sand about 250 miles away which had been slightly flattened in the desert. All it had was a tent or two, a few bombs and some petrol. We were to land there, top up our fuel and then fly on to the target, Benghazi, another 450 miles further where the target was the usual one, shipping in the harbour.

The first leg of the trip was a straightforward flight in daylight across the delta to the stretch of sand, L106. I was feeling a little tired after the previous evening, so I told the crew that there were not likely to be any problems, as it was daylight, we were not flying at any great height and visibility was good, so I would take a nap on the bed with which all Wimpies were equipped and they should wake me up if there were any problems.

The next thing I knew was being awakened to be told that there was a minor sandstorm and the pilot could not see anything on the ground. When the storm cleared we found ourselves over the sea, which was not part of the plan at all. We altered course to the south-west until we hit the coast, flew inland until we found the landing strip, landed and refuelled and took off again for the target. The run to the harbour of Benghazi was straightforward and we arrived at about midnight. The area was very heavily defended with light and heavy anti-aircraft guns, as it was regularly bombed, so the flak was intense over the target.

We made our run with the crew's regular observer doing the bombing, got the bombs away, and then the Wimpy was hit by something pretty hefty in the starboard engine. At the same time, the observer was hit in the head by a piece of shrapnel which left him semi-conscious, with blood streaming down his face and neck. We covered his wound with a field dressing and got him back to the bed.

I took over the navigation and suggested to the pilot that as we now had only one engine, we should fly back along the coast where a forced landing, if it became necessary, could be made on the beach, an impossibility inland among the mountains and very rough desert which stretched for the next hundred miles or so. It was well known that the Germans had captured and were using several British aircraft, and that as a result, the gunners defending Tobruk were 'flak-happy', firing at any aircraft in sight. As we neared Tobruk, we fired off the colours of the day, but they still shot at us, causing the pilot to weave; fortunately, he avoided our being hit again. By now our remaining engine was working erratically and we were losing height. At about 1500 feet we approached the Bay of Sollum where the planned route would have meant a dog-leg round the bay, so we decided to cut across the bay.

We wanted to get past the front line which was at Sollum, and the pilot ordered us into ditching positions as the port engine was decidedly ropey. This meant that the wireless operator, the front gunner, the injured observer on the bed and I were all behind the main spar, and it was my duty to have my hand on the dinghy release. The pilot said he would take the Very pistol if we had to ditch, and I put all the spare cartridges for it inside my jacket. The observer had by now recovered consciousness, although he was still not very well.

We had gradually been losing height over the bay, and suddenly we hit the water at over a hundred miles an hour. It was like hitting concrete. The injured observer sat up with the force of the sudden stop, and everything not fastened down shot forward, including the Elsan closet, (portable toilet), which broke loose from its mooring at the rear of the aircraft and hit him on the back of the head. Not only was he knocked unconscious again, but he was covered in rather unpleasant things. I remembered to release the dinghy. The pilot squeezed out through the escape hatch above his head and did a spectacular dive into the water. The rear gunner climbed out from his turret and then the front gunner, the wireless operator and I poured the unconscious observer out through the astrodome and helped him to the dinghy.

Wellingtons (Wimpies) are supposed to float for a considerable time, but the automatic flotation gear must have been hit by the flak and this one sank in less than two minutes. The dinghy was self-inflating, and one of the early circular types, but was only two-thirds inflated. We all managed to help each other into the dinghy, although at two o'clock in the morning it was still quite dark.

We took stock of our situation. We had two non-swimmers and an unconscious man. As for the equipment, we had plugs for mending any holes in the dinghy, yellow dye to spread on the sea to mark our situation for any air-sea rescue plane that might appear, chewing gum, Horlicks tablets and chocolate marked, 'Emergency Only. To be opened only in the presence of an officer'. This had the property of binding up one's innards and so avoiding hunger pangs if one were short of food. There was a hot water bottle supposedly full of brandy for emergencies, some morphine ampoules, a small First Aid kit, two water bottles, a hand mirror, two 'Signals Distress Marine' and, of course, all my cartridges. I checked with the pilot whether he had the Very pistol. He had lost it when he did his dive into the water from the plane. Without the pistol there was no way of firing the cartridges to send signals with, so there was nothing we could do until daylight.

While it was still quite dark we discovered that the dinghy was deflating. There was a pump built into the dinghy, but when we tried it, nothing happened, and we found that the pump junction was unserviceable and so useless.

We sat out the rest of the night and when at dawn we saw the usual Hurricane of the Photographic Reconnaissance Unit coming from the East and flying westwards to go and take photos of the damage we had done in the raid, I grabbed one of the Signals, Distress Marine. These had a tape on the top which, when pulled sharply, should ignite a little rocket. I had used these before, in practice, so I pulled as required, but nothing happened, and the Hurricane disappeared in the distance.

As it was now getting daylight, we decided to put out the yellow dye, so that we would be visible to anyone looking for us. By now the observer was becoming delirious, and we thought that a drop of brandy might help. I opened the hot water bottle, sniffed it, and because it did not smell like brandy, I tasted it. Someone had 'borrowed' the brandy and replaced it with water. The poor chap seemed to calm down somewhat after a shot of morphine.

By now the P.R.U. Hurricane was on the return journey and on its appearance I 'operated' the second Signals Distress Marine. You can guess what happened. Nothing! The light was now improving and we found we could see the coast. It appeared to be about three or four miles away and we decided that if the worst came to the worst, whoever could swim the best should try to reach land. The pilot was an Australian, and like most of them, could swim very well. I could certainly swim three or four miles in those days, and so we agreed that if need arose, we would both go.

It was daylight by now, and the wireless operator, who was of course the expert in Morse Code, flashed 'SOS' to the shore with the hand mirror, in the hope of attracting someone's attention. Almost immediately we had a reply which the W/Op translated as 'Cheer up, boys, help is coming.' The sea was becoming rather choppy, three of the fellows were seasick and the dinghy was still deflating. Those of us who could swim now took turns out in the sea, to help the dinghy ride higher out of the water for the benefit of the others.

After some time, a Wimpy appeared in the East, and started to fly a square search over the bay, which is the standard way of looking for a lost aircraft. After a number of squares, during which he seemed at times to be going further and further away, the pilot found us, to our great delight. His Wimpy did a terrific dive from about 5000 feet and 'beat us up', but the idiot had left his trailing aerial out; this is a long wire with 30 or 40 small lead weights on the tail, and it should always be reeled in at low altitudes. He must have forgotten in the excitement of finding us, and it hit the water about six feet away from the dinghy. Had the wire hit it, it would have cut the dinghy in two, and probably us as well. We waved, pointed to our mouths, and he climbed, then dropped various parcels of supplies and another dinghy to us. Unfortunately, he dropped them from too great a height, and they all sank, except the dinghy. We swimmers swam the 50 yards or so to it and towed it back. It was a Mark 1 dinghy of triangular shape, also with a built-in pump, which also proved to be broken. So we now had two partly-inflated dinghies, which was an improvement on one partly-inflated dinghy.

The Wimpy then flew off, waving to us, and we assumed that somewhere the wheels were turning. Those of us in the water occupied the second dinghy. Some time later, we heard aircraft noise, coming from the north. North of us, we knew, was Crete, which was occupied by the Germans, and our dinghy was surrounded by yellow dye. Our thoughts were, 'My God, if they see us they will shoot us out of the water.' When they appeared, we could see small single-engined planes. '109s' we thought. On closer inspection they proved to be Hurricanes, escorting a Walrus, which is an amphibious aircraft. The Hurricanes then disappeared, and the Walrus stooged around before dropping a smoke float, so that they could get the direction of the wind in order to decide landing direction, and that missed us by only a very few feet indeed. The Walrus touched down on the rather choppy sea and taxied alongside, Our pilot stood up, and was hit on the back of the neck by the float on the wing of the Walrus. Now we had two unconscious bodies.

With some effort and the assistance of the crew of the Walrus, we managed to get the unconscious men on board, and the rest of us all climbed in. The Walrus is not a large aeroplane, but somehow the six of us and their crew of three squeezed in. The plane was by now grossly overloaded, and the pilot doubted that he would be able to get her off the water. In fact, it proved impossible, and after a couple of attempts, he gave up and we taxied to the shore, where the pilot put his wheels down and ran up on to the beach. We later found out that the distance we had thought of swimming was in fact eleven miles; had we tried to swim, we probably would not have made it.

There to greet us on the beach was a crowd of South African Army types who made us most welcome, took us into a tent and asked us what we would like to eat. I facetiously said, 'Steak and chips and some Scotch will do.' They promised to do what they could, and within about ten minutes they brought in - steak and chips and brandy! It transpired that they had shot a desert buck that morning and had cut us some steaks from it; they had sweet potatoes from which they had made us chips, and of course, South Africans are always well supplied with brandy.

I asked who had signalled a reply to our SOS, and was told that they had used their heliograph. When I saw it I was astonished to find that it was a large desert heliograph of about

18 inch diameter. It had seemed just a pinprick of light to us, but we had been eleven miles away. We were later taken into their First Aid tent to meet one of their soldiers who had been on the beach when the Wimpy had come over and 'beat them up', still with its trailing aerial out, and his left shoulder had been smashed.

That night we were given beds in tents, and woke up some hours later to find shells falling all round us; we spent the rest of the night in slit trenches. Next morning the South Africans kindly drove us along the coast to Sidi Barrani, from where we were able to contact Kabrit, who arranged for our transport back to base. Thus ended the day on which almost everything went wrong, - but all's well that ends well. The result was that I became a member of the Goldfish Club, membership of which is restricted to those who have saved their lives by the use of a dinghy.

Chapter 11

MINES and BOMBS

On one occasion we were detailed to lay mines in Benghazi harbour, which was a fairly dicey experience as it meant flying very low over the water at a steady speed. The moles of the harbour were packed with light anti-aircraft guns which were able to depress their aim at their target – us! We returned from the trip to be told by the de-briefing officer that what we had so carefully laid in the harbour were sandbags! Anger and consternation ensued until it was pointed out that Jerry spotted the splashes when mines were laid and then went out and swept them. They of course could find no mines, and we heard later that we had closed the harbour for two days.

Later on, the Station Commander decided that as Observers were the ones who dropped the bombs, they should help the armourers in bombing-up the aircraft. On one occasion I had just completed my chore of helping load my Wimpy with 4000 lbs of assorted mayhem and was in the bomb-aiming position, (prone), checking my bomb-sight when an erk, probably a fitter, crouched down beside me and enquired how we were able to drop our loads in sticks if we did not wish to drop salvoes.

I explained about the gadget we called the Mickey Mouse which allowed us to select crater distance automatically and pointed it out to him. 'Oh!' said the laddie. 'It's nothing to do with this then?' and pushed the jettison bar. This was of course for emergency use if we wished to get rid of our bomb-load in a hurry – which it did! It is impossible to compute the speed at which I left the aircraft but fortunately nothing exploded – except the Station Commander who had just driven up on a tour of inspection. The unfortunate airman was duly posted – where I do not know.

Another bomb incident occurred when we received two new aircraft with bomb-bays modified to carry the Cookie – the 4000 lb blockbuster shaped rather like two dustbins welded together. All Observers were instructed to attend a demonstration by the Flight-Sergeant Armourer to show how to load the monster. This we did and were shown how to raise it into the bomb-bay by means of a special winch. 'There you are,' said the Chiefy, 'piece of cake! Now it's rock-solid.' To prove this he gave the 4000 pounder a hefty whack – and it fell to earth with a mighty thump. I am sure many world records for the hundred yard sprint were broken but again the Gods smiled upon me and there was no explosion.

Chapter 12

DOUBLE TROUBLE

My thirteenth Middle East 'op.' was somewhat memorable. The squadron, together with what seemed to be the rest of the Middle East Air Force, was detailed to use El Adem airfield, a fairly flat piece of sand near Tobruk, as assembly point for an attack on the Italian fleet in the Med. An aircraft equipped with A.S.V. (Anti Surface Vessel equipment) was to shadow the fleet and would send signals for us, the bomber force, to 'home' on. Our Wimpies were loaded with A.P. and S.A.P. (armour piercing and semi-armour piercing) bombs and we were given the latitude and longitude of the last known position of the fleet. We were to fly to this point, listening out for signals from the A.S.V. aircraft. On reaching the given latitude and longitude of the last known position of the enemy fleet we should start 'square searching' for it. If we sighted it we were to drop flares and then attack.

Before take-off we had to wait for the latest meteorological report which would give us a wind speed and direction with which to start our navigation. We waited and we waited and we waited and eventually the forecast came – 'Winds light and variable', a forecast which gave us so little information as to be of no help at all to us.

My aircraft was the last of our squadron to take off and we

proceeded to the bit of the Mediterranean as directed. We heard nothing from the shadowing aircraft and proceeded with our square search. Then, still having seen no flares and heard no signals, we pressed on to our point of no return, that is, the limit set by our available fuel, and returned to El Adem still carrying our full bomb load. The landing was smooth and uneventful until a tyre burst and the Wimpy ground-looped. We, the crew, must have broken all known speed records leaving the wreckage, which was a good thing as it went up with a very large bang.

A new problem now presented itself. How were we to get back to our base at Kabrit? All the rest of our squadron had left for home. However we managed to persuade a crew from 37 Squadron, stationed on the western side of the Great Bitter Lake, to give us a lift. On getting near the lake we talked the 37 Sqn. bods into landing at Kabrit, thus saving our having to organise transport if we had landed at their base. I was standing in the astrodome while their second pilot was landing and it seemed to me that we were travelling rather faster than was usual for a normal landing. My fears proved to be right, unfortunately. We ran off the end of the runway at a very high rate of knots, through a couple of tents, fortunately uninhabited and not 'dug in', and performed another ground loop. This was becoming monotonous. Luckily no-one was seriously hurt, but as it was my thirteenth op. the whole thing was obviously my fault, so I had to buy the beer.

Chapter 13

OLD PALS

Whilst I was spending some time at one of our advanced landing grounds I received a signal from RAF headquarters in Cairo, signed Sergeant Gilbert Christie, asking me to call in and see him in the A.O.C. in C's office in Cairo. I had known Gilbert before the war and that he was a highly qualified shorthand-typist who had suffered from mastoid trouble, due, it was thought, to his having been a keen and very successful schoolboy boxer. We had both worked for the Brighton Corporation Electricity Undertaking, and we used to go swimming near the pier each lunchtime, travelling on my BSA 250 motorbike. I remembered that he had wanted to join the R.A.F. but I knew that he would have not been fit enough for aircrew.

It so happened that a week or so later I had to go with an aircraft to Heliopolis (near Cairo) for an engine change. I had expected to return to the desert immediately but on arriving at Helio was informed that it would be at least two days before I could get back to the A.L.G. Although I was in scruff order - I didn't even have a forage cap with me, only my flying helmet - I thought I would take the opportunity of trying to see my old friend Gilbert. I managed to get to M.E.H.Q. in Cairo but was almost in trouble with the S.P.s (Service Police) for being improperly dressed. I explained my position and managed to persuade them to ring Gilbert's office. He soon sorted things out and invited me in. It turned out that he was the A.O.C. in C's personal clerk and thus was able to examine squadron records, which was how he managed to find me. I believe he ended the war as a Wing Commander.

I had been in Gilbert's office only a few minutes when the door opened and in came a not very tall figure with pilot's wings, umpteen gongs and more rank braid than I had ever seen before. It was Air Vice Marshal Tedder, the A.O.C. in C., R.A.F. Middle East, virtually God himself!

I leapt to attention expecting at least to be shot at dawn for my unairmanlike appearance, only to be greeted with the words, 'Good morning, Sergeant. I see you are down from the desert. What squadron are you with?'

'Good morning, sir, I'm with 148 Squadron.'

'Ah, Turkey Rainsford's lot. Give him my compliments when you return and tell him that I shall be visiting you very shortly.'

My C.O., Wing Commander Rainsford was affectionately known to all as 'Turkey', but we understood that he was not too enamoured of the nickname. I was then offered a drink by AVM Tedder, who pointed out that it would have to be orange juice so early in the day and then asked if I smoked. I replied that I smoked a pipe and was immediately offered the AVM's personal pouch. I found all through my service career that the higher the rank, the more human the people were.

That evening Gilbert and I treated ourselves to a meal at the then famous (and very expensive) Groppi's restaurant. Gilbert had lent me some clean uniform and organised a bath and a shave for me. We were just finishing a fine repast when another pre-war friend of mine walked in. They say it's a small world, don't they? Philip Pearce was some ten years older than I was, and had been an industrial chemist. He was now in the uniform of a Flying Officer but apparently flew a desk, as he wore no brevet. He did not have very good eyesight. He told us that he had recently qualified as a Meteorological Officer and had been posted to R.A.F. Heliopolis. He had a wonderful line-shoot to tell us. On his first day there he was walking back from the Mess to Station H.Q. with his Commanding Officer when the C.O. said, 'That's an odd looking cloud formation there, Pearce. What does it mean to you?'

'According to the book, it should rain within about half an hour, sir,' replied Philip.

It had not rained in Helio in the memory of the C.O. but lo and behold! After about twenty minutes there was a short sharp downpour!

Philip thereafter could do no wrong, but he told us that it was a difficult reputation to live up to.

Chapter 14

LATE ARRIVALS CLUB

It was the Milk Run again. Benghazi was the main supply port for Rommel and his Afrika Korps and our target was shipping and the harbour installations. Navigationally it was not a difficult operation. The Squadron had attacked B.G. so often that there must have been a groove worn in the sky for us to fly in.

We arrived at the target with no mishap, but on the bombing run a lucky (or I suppose I should say unlucky) flak shell did our starboard engine no good at all. Jimmy, the driver, was unable to maintain height and ordered the jettisoning of everything movable. A Wimpy can usually fly quite well on one engine but the port one began missing occasionally. We, the rest of the crew, had thrown overboard all that we could and it was now up to Jimmy to do his best to keep us airborne.

Now comes my big line-shoot. I was looking out of the astro-hatch and could see land *above* me on both sides! This had never happened to me before. We were flying in a valley. Unfortunately it was a cul-de-sac, and with no warning the Wimpy hit the mountain at the end at something over 100 miles an hour. The kite rolled about a quarter of a mile downhill, snapping off both wings. The body of the fuselage remained intact, thanks to the Wimpy's geodetic construction, in which the stresses are distributed within the structure itself by means of skeletal struts. We were tossed about like peas in a drum, until we finally came to a halt. I was still able to move and we were trying to extricate ourselves from the wreckage when I heard Ginger, the wireless operator, yell, 'Look out! My set's on fire!' There were several hundred gallons of highly flammable fuel strewn down the mountainside, which could have caused a major problem. Fortunately a few seconds later the cry was, 'It's gone out!' and many sighs of relief were breathed.

We now had to get ourselves together and make plans for the immediate future. The two pilots, front gunner, wireless op and myself, (the observer), were present and fairly correct, bruised and somewhat bloody, but there was no sign of Tony, our rear-gunner. The fuselage was non-existent beyond the flare-chute. No tail unit – no rear gun-turret! It was very dark – it was about 01.00 hours – so we started searching for Tony as best we could. I found the rear gun-turret about 200 yards away, and on feeling inside could find nothing. Geoff, our front gunner, found Tony about 200 yards away in the opposite direction. He was unconscious, his nose badly broken and bleeding badly. We patched him up as best we could, and started to take stock of our situation. We were approximately 300 miles behind enemy lines so we had a long walk in prospect.

Our first priority was water. We each had individual water bottles, but they had been stowed at the rear of the aircraft, which was no longer there. The large emergency water tank, a metal cylinder about three feet long and fifteen inches in diameter, was still in place, but on examining it we found it had been badly holed, probably by the flak. It had about a gallon in it still, and that was all the water we had. We managed to wrench it from what remained of the fuselage, so we had at least a little water to sustain us, although the tank was rather difficult to carry. We also had our 'for use in emergencies only' chocolate, which we knew was intended to 'bind' us, and supposedly help ward off hunger pangs. We still had our 'flying rations' – chocolate bars and Horlicks tablets which I had kept in my Navigation bag. Tony had by this time regained consciousness, and was 'in fair condition'. We all had aches and pains and quite severe bruising. I personally had very painful ribs and left ankle, but our first priority was to get away from the scene of the prang as quickly as possible, for we did not know how close the nearest Jerries were. We therefore set off in as easterly direction as possible, the general direction in which our base lay.

We walked for the rest of the night and just before dawn we came to a road running east to west which had traffic on it. We hid in some convenient bushes until it was safe to cross. Many of the vehicles we saw were laden with troops, whom we had no desire to meet. There were again some convenient bushes on the other side of the road, in which we concealed ourselves until the whole crew were across. Geoff, the front gunner, was last over, and just as he joined us, a large Jerry truck approached and *stopped*! A 'nature call' was obviously required by the passengers, and we must have held our collective breaths for about five minutes while silently praying that none of the 'relieving troops' would wander too close to us. Fortunately none did, and we hurried away from that road as quickly as possible after the truck had proceeded on its way.

We were taking turns at carrying the water tank. There was no other container available. A rather hurried search for our individual water bottles had proved fruitless and the future provision of water was our greatest concern. We knew that we could survive for some considerable time without food, but the need for water was another matter.

The terrain was by now changing rapidly. As we left the uplands the surface became much drier and very stony indeed – not nice rounded pebbles but sharp pieces of rock, and the 'soil' was becoming rather sandy. Our footwear was not the most suitable for this kind of hiking. We were all wearing soft and rather loose fleecy-lined suede flying boots – fine for keeping the feet warm at umpteen thousand feet, but NOT for walking any distance under such conditions as we were experiencing. I have always suffered from 'sissy' feet. I could not even walk on shingle on an English beach without some footwear, and my feet were already becoming quite uncomfortable.

We spent the next night huddled together in a wadi – a dried-up river bed – and believe me, at night, the sands of the desert really do grow cold. During that night a minor miracle occurred. There was a short sharp shower of rain. We had no means of collecting any of this, but the next morning we could lap at puddles. One will do anything when one is really thirsty. The rain had also caused a few thistles to appear and we found that their 'fruit' part was quite edible. We slogged on for the rest of that day and spent another cold night mostly complaining about the low temperature. By this time we had eaten all our flying rations as well as the dreaded emergency chocolate.

The following morning we set off again eastwards and after about an hour we met a lone Arab, on foot. He appeared friendly and when we asked for water – we had a little Arabic between us – he led us to a small concealed well, about three-quarters of an hour's walk away. We quenched our thirsts and were trying to replenish the water in the water tank when the Arab, who had said he was a Senussi, insisted that we take his leather water bottle, which he had refilled. He then persuaded us to follow him and he signed that we would be able to get some food. The Senussi then set off at a great rate of knots, and we had to show him that we could not walk at his pace. After a couple of hours, during which we had several rests, we came to his camp and were introduced to the sheik. This worthy spoke some very limited English and we were able to converse reasonably satisfactorily. We knew that the Senussi were an Arab tribe who had been very badly treated by the Italians on account of the Senussi having spearheaded the revolutionary movement against the Italian colonisation of Cyrenaica. They were therefore pro-British.

We had to go through the rather long and complicated Arab coffee ceremony, while the fatted calf (kid, actually) was slaughtered to provide us with a meal. It turned out to be a kind of stew and I for some reason had been given the honour of having the creature's eyes in my portion, which I found staring at me as I reached the bottom of my dish. I am afraid I let the side down badly by dashing behind the tent and being violently sick.

That night was somewhat more comfortable as we were given blankets or rugs to keep ourselves warm. The next morning the Senussi gave us the Arab version of breakfast and then told us that there were some white soldiers over the hill who were not German or Italian and that a guide would take us to them. We were given some dried dates and a sort of pemmican or biltong (dried meat) to take with us, and we did our best to thank our host by giving him half our cigarettes – I think we all smoked except Jimmy – and a note 'to whom it may concern' saying that the sheik had been of great assistance to British Aircrew in enemy territory. We then set off with our original contact, who again had to be persuaded not to attempt Olympic records. 'Over the hill' was obviously a Senussi figure of speech. We went over many hills, again with numerous enforced rest periods, but eventually, just before dusk we came upon a group of British soldiers in a wadi. These turned out to be about a dozen members of the famed Long Range Desert Group who had been ferried up behind Jerry lines to observe troop movements and indulge in the odd spot of sabotage. They were due to be picked up the next day at a rendezvous which was a disused well-cum-waterhole some miles away. They had plenty of rations and fed us with bully-beef, biscuits and tea. Not exactly Cordon Bleu but infinitely more palatable than goat's eyes.

By now, we airmen in our suede flying boots were really having trouble with our feet. Mine were bleeding quite badly and I was not looking forward to a long march in that condition. I pointed this out to their senior officer and he got their medical orderly to apply ointment and bandages which gave me some relief.

The next morning an Arab appeared with a camel to carry the L.R.D.G. equipment and it was decided that I should pilot the thing as my feet were almost too painful to stand on. Anyone who has ever ridden any distance on a camel will know why it is called the ship of the desert. It was the nearest thing I had ever been to seasick in my life. The strange motion of the beast has to be experienced to be believed, but nevertheless it was better than walking. After several hours we reached the rendezvous and sat around to await the arrival of the L.R.D.G. transport.

The odd Arab was now joining our group and one brought a message that 'a traitor' had betrayed us to the Germans. Our chief concern then was whether they, the Jerry, would arrive before the L.R.D.G. transport. We were deployed in defensive positions round the dried up waterhole. The R.A.F. were armed with spare L.R.D.G. weapons, and Tony and I were detailed to stay in the old waterhole – a sort of underground cave – with two hand-grenades each as the last line of defence. Not really the sort of thing we had been trained for. Someone called to us that some transport had been sighted and that the passengers looked like Afrika Korps. Suddenly a shot rang out from one of our group. Much heart-in-mouth feeling! A few moments later we were told that all was O.K. – they were our chaps after all. It turned out that one of 'our' Arabs was a little trigger happy and had loosed off the shot we had heard. Fortunately the bods on the gharries (a Service name for any kind of transport in the Middle East) did not return the fire. They were equipped with 0.5 calibre machine-guns which would have done us no good at all.

There were three trucks which were returning to Siwa Oasis, the L.R.D.G. base way down south in the desert, after depositing the replacement men. The navigator was a large Maori sergeant (aren't all Maori fellows large?) and I managed to get myself on to his vehicle, because as a navigator myself I was naturally very interested in his technique. Navigation by motor vehicle in the desert has two parts – a 'dead reckoning' course by compass and speedometer, and an 'astro-fix' by observation of stars or sun to check the accuracy of the D.R. position. A magnetic compass is not much use in a vehicle made of metal. The magnetism of shifting loads, changing gear wheels and varying engine speeds makes the compass almost impossible to compensate accurately; the only way to get a correct bearing is to stop and walk a few yards from the vehicle. On their long journeys it would have meant frequent delays, so the L.R.D.G. used sun-compasses whenever the sun shone, and occasionally in moonlight. The sun-compass was ideal for the job. Without worrying about the induced magnetism of the truck or the earth's magnetic field, it gave directly the true bearing which was then plotted on the map. The sun-compass consists of a horizontal circle, divided into 360 degrees with a central needle casting a shadow across the graduations rather like a sundial. The circle is fixed to the dashboard of the car, and by rotating the circle throughout the day to correspond with the sun's movement through the sky, the shadow is made to indicate the true bearing on which the vehicle is travelling.

For the astro-fix observations the L.R.D.G. used theodolites. In an aircraft at night when we (the navigators) took star shots with a bubble sextant, we needed to compute our results quickly on account of the speed we were travelling. There was not quite such a rush for the desert navigator. He could be stationary to take his shots, which no doubt enhanced their accuracy.

Our journey by trucks to Siwa Oasis, the L.R.D.G. base about 300 miles further south in the desert, was somewhat easier than walking. It took us about 24 hours. We had a very interesting journey, gingerly driving through German minefields, and looking for petrol caches which the L.R.D.G. had hidden and which needed pin-point navigational expertise to find. En route we crossed enemy lines. The track we were on crossed the lines and the barbed wire had already been cut, possibly by the L.R.D.G. on one of their earlier journeys. It was out in the wilderness, far from any enemy bases, fortunately.

On our arrival at the Long Range Desert Group base an Army medical officer checked us over, dosed us to get rid of the effect of our 'special' chocolate and attended to our various injuries and bruises. I had a chipped ankle bone and two cracked ribs.

After a couple of days – mostly spent in agony trying to get rid of the 'chocolate' – a Bombay aircraft came to take us back to base at Kabrit on the Great Bitter Lake.

Thus we became members of the Late Arrivals Club, membership of which is open only to those returning from behind enemy lines and avoiding capture. The badge, unofficial, of course, was a flying boot with a wing attached. This was the second of the clubs which I had not the least desire to join, but which fate decreed that I should.

We discovered some months later that we had all been 'Mentioned in Despatches' for our efforts and success in returning to active service through enemy lines.

Unkempt, unshaven! Taken immediately on return from long walk back across the North African desert, through enemy lines. Kabrit 1942 (Photo by Howard Hewer). D. Egles 3rd from left.

Chapter 15

A NON-LUXURY CRUISE

The powers that be at Kabrit decided that I should have a break from operational flying for a bit and sent me to Landing Ground 104, a strip of fairly smooth sand in the desert which was used as an advanced base for the Squadron, to carry out various duties. These included airfield maintenance, (dragging a grader behind a lorry to level out the bumps on the landing strip), duty pilot, which was really air traffic control by communicating with incoming aircraft by means of the TR9 radio, (a short range equipment all our aircraft were equipped with), to give permission to land after operational sorties, as well as various odd jobs like checking on the fuel supply and the contents of the bomb dump.

After some weeks of this I was told that 'they' were asking for volunteer observers and pilots to go to Canada to ferry Liberator aircraft across the Atlantic to Britain. As there seemed to be little hope of my going back on operational flying for a while, I volunteered and was accepted. Those of us who had opted for this interesting sounding duty were photographed for 'civvy' passports and measured for 'civvy' suits for some reason that I never was able to fathom. We never saw suits or passports!

A most interesting journey ensued. We were driven down to Suez, some thirty-odd of us, where we embarked on the *Queen*

Mary, at that time the largest passenger vessel in the world. She had been used as a troopship for some time, and cabins that were designed to carry two passengers had been converted to take at least eight. On enquiring about our fellow passengers we were informed that accompanying us were some three thousand Afrika Korps prisoners together with two thousand Polish troops acting as their guards.

Our route was Suez, Durban, Cape Town, Rio de Janeiro and New York, but it was not exactly a luxurious pleasure cruise. After a couple of days it was decided that everybody would have to do guard duty and this we did. At first we were armed with our usual .38 revolvers, then we were given .303 rifles, but these proved to be unwieldy in ship passageways so we were issued with Italian rifles which had built-in bayonets.

These looked like toys after the British .303s, but we found out after a few practice rounds fired out to sea that the 'toys' had kicks like cantankerous mules. At the end of each passageway between cabins the Poles had machine-guns mounted and we hoped that none of them had itchy fingers.

Although the German prisoners were sleeping in the lowest decks they had of course to come on to higher decks for exercise and we were amazed to see how smart many of them appeared. We understood that they used part of their butter ration as hairdressing.

The *Queen Mary* was officially 'dry', but we managed to get some beer aboard at Suez, although sad to say it had run out long before we reached Durban. We were not able to replenish our stock for the rest of our journey and the only refreshment available was the ubiquitous Coca-Cola. That trip put me off Coke for years.

Halfway across the Atlantic the Afrika Korps men tried to set fire to the vessel – unsuccessfully, thank goodness, and at Rio de

Janeiro about half-a-dozen jumped overboard and swam ashore but the Brazilian police were vigilant and returned them to the ship.

We eventually arrived at New York, where were met by what looked like half the United States Army and the whole of the New York Police Force. I have never seen so many sub-machine-guns in my life.

On board we had been able to purchase cigarettes at shipboard prices and I had virtually filled my parachute bag (which all aircrew used as personal kit carriers) and was hoping that U.S. Customs would not be too hard on me.

I was walking through the dock gates, having seen no Customs officials, when I was stopped by a police officer who examined the outside of my parachute bag, noticed that it had not the statutory chalk cross on and directed me to the nearby Customs shed. Oh dear I thought, this is it. and put my bag up on the counter. 'Don't open that, bud!' came a shout and a Customs Officer dashed across and hurriedly decorated my bag with the much needed chalk cross, showed me the door and expressed the hope that I would enjoy my stay in the States.

Chapter 16

CANADA and U.S.A.

We aircrew types were quickly gathered up and put on a train to Canada. In the dining car that evening I saw the biggest steak I had ever seen served to one of my colleagues, and I thought that South Africa served some monsters. This one overflowed a full-sized dinner plate – quite a change from the (often) liquid bully beef of the desert. Rationing had certainly not arrived in the North Americas.

The next day we arrived at Lachine in Quebec, were given billets and we observers were told to report next morning to the Navigation section. There an R.C.A.F. Flying Officer met us, and started to give us *very* basic navigation lessons. We endured this for about half an hour and then pointed out that we had forgotten gen of that standard ages ago and felt that having completed at least one tour of operations we did not need to be reminded of such elementary information. The instructor asked us where we had come from and on being informed that we had come straight from operational squadrons in the Western Desert, he said he would have to consult a senior officer. He then dismissed us. We were later informed that 'they' – the powers that be, were no longer ferrying Liberators to Britain but only to North Africa and we were not to be sent back there but we would wait for a sea passage back to England.

We had nothing to do, officially, so some of us wandered into the town of Lachine for a drink, only to discover to our absolute horror that the place was 'dry'. Some R.C.A.F bods we asked told us that if a drink was required the form was to get in a taxi and say 'Bootlegger, please.' One would be taken to a liquor supplier where a purchase could be made which one would consume in an hotel room booked for the afternoon or evening. This information proved to be absolutely true. After a couple of days we were told that we could apply for seven days leave, so four of us, one of whom was Peter Fullerton, asked for travel warrants to New York. We had to visit the Station Warrant Officer to complete formalities and draw some money, and as I was putting my dollars into my wallet the S.W.O. noticed in it a couple of postage stamps which I had bought on Malta during the siege. He said that he was a keen philatelist and would like to purchase one or both of them. As they were of no value or importance to me I said that he could have them as a gift. On hearing that we were going to New York, he told me that a great friend of his, Xavier Cugat, the then famous band leader, was also a stamp fanatic and that if I would like to deliver the other stamp to him he would be most grateful. The S.W.O. gave me a note of introduction to Xavier Cugat.

On arriving in New York we booked into the hotel in Times Square that had Billy Rose's Diamond Horseshoe nightclub on its premises – I believe that it was called the Paramount. The season was midsummer and we found it very hot indeed in N.Y., although we had only recently left the Western Desert. We still had our khaki-drill uniforms and we decided that that would be the thing to wear, so we donned our khaki shorts and long socks and put on our K.D. tunics which carried our rank and flying brevets. We had not strolled far round Times Square before we found ourselves the centre of much attention particularly from the female sex. This of course did not bother us too much until we were approached by a large police officer who wanted to know why were dressed in such a disgusting manner. On looking at each other we then realised that we were wearing our tunics over our desert shorts, which were not the issue R.A.F. length but had been considerably shortened and were almost completely covered by the tunics. We did look, as the police officer said, 'pantless'. He advised us to 'Get some proper pants on' so we returned to the hotel to get dressed in long trousers. On the way were stopped by a couple of American G.I.s who said that they wished they had similar uniforms!

We spent the rest of the day 'rubbernecking' – one's first visit to New York is rather breathtaking. We went up the Empire State Building which was then the highest building in the world and were suitably impressed, and that evening we found the hotel where Xavier Cugat was performing and managed to get my Maltese stamp delivered to him. He was most grateful and invited us in, insisting on treating us all to copious draughts of the very best champagne. On Broadway we discovered the famous Stage Door Canteen which was run for the benefit of Service personnel by the U.S.O., the United Services Organisation, and often manned by 'stars of stage screen and radio'. While we were in there we were given free passes to the Radio City Music Hall – an enormous cinema – and an athletic club invited us to dinner, where we were entertained very well indeed.

Next afternoon we visited the Radio City Music Hall, where the main feature film was *Mrs Miniver* with Greer Garson. Outside the cinema there was an extremely long queue and we four tacked ourselves on to the end of it. We edged forward slowly with all the other folk until a commissionaire approached us with the words, 'What are you guys doing there? Come with me.'

Clutching our free tickets we followed him with some trepidation, not knowing what we had done wrong. Perhaps we were in the incorrect queue? Not a bit of it! He took us into the main entrance, ahead of all the cash customers, and ushered us to very good seats. Service personnel, even foreigners, were treated very well in the U.S.A., especially when there was a war on. Of course, in those days, a cinema programme did not consist of just the main film, plus a second feature film, plus a cartoon, but also a first class stage show. The famous Rockettes, a seemingly endless chorus line on one of the largest stages I have ever seen, danced for our entertainment, and we had, particularly for me, a 'big band' fan, the pleasure of a concert by Charlie Barnett and his Orchestra. Perhaps some of my more elderly readers remember 'Skyliner', his signature tune?

Somehow the word got to the band-leader that there were some 'Limeys' in the audience and we were invited back to Charlie Barnett's studio for snacks and drinks and much talk about jazz and 'big-band' music.

The next day we again visited the U.S.O., and one of the ladies chatting to us remarked that it must be very expensive at the hotel we were staying at, and that she could get us far better terms at the Vanderbilt Hotel.

This was arranged and we saved ourselves a considerable amount of money. This lady also noticed my metal winged boot badge that I was wearing and enquired what it meant. I explained that it was the unofficial badge of the Late Arrivals Club and she was quite impressed. We were invited to an athletic club party in the evening which was followed by a dance. During this my partner and I won the modern waltz competition. I am no Victor Sylvester so I am sure the award was fixed. On the following day we sent our K.D. (khaki drill) uniforms to be laundered and they were returned in two hours, but minus the buttons! On complaining, we were informed that the laundresses had taken them as souvenirs and we had to explain that we could not possibly replace the buttons in New York, or indeed in the whole U.S.A., and that we would be in serious trouble if we reported for duty buttonless, whereupon they were returned to us.

On visiting the U.S.O. again that day I was told by the lady who had admired my Late Arrivals Club badge that she had arranged for me to be photographed at the Rockefeller Centre for *Vogue*, the female fashion magazine. On our arrival there, the photographer met us, and he turned out to be an Englishman living in the States but who came from Worthing in Sussex. As I lived in Hove, we were practically neighbours. We were taken onto a roof-garden and surrounded by about a dozen police officers, most of whom carried Tommy-guns. Then two or three gorgeous girls appeared swathed in diamonds. We were informed that about a million dollars worth of 'ice' was on show. This explained the heavy police presence.

After the photo session, George, the photographer said to us, 'I know what you guys need. Come with me!' and he led us out to his enormous motor-car and proceeded to drive to East umpty-umph street, stopping outside a window with 'Mike's Place' in very large letters across the window – straight out of all the best gangster movies. We went inside to be greeted by a very large Irish-American, obviously Mike himself, to whom we were introduced. 'I know what you guys want. Hang on,' he said and disappeared into the nether regions to reappear clutching two cobwebby crates which were full of bottled Guinness. Nectar, after the average American brew. As I said before, this was August in N.Y. and the temperature and humidity were both high so we settled in to do our best to empty the crates. If my memory serves me correctly, we managed to do this.

The only problem was that our new-found friend George became rather the worse for wear. When we got him out into the comparatively fresh air he collapsed completely. We poured him into the back of his convertible – the hood was down – and I was elected to drive the monster back to the Rockefeller Centre. (I suppose I should spell that Center). George had explained to us that if you travel at exactly thirty miles per hour you will not hit a red light and I wished to try and prove the correctness of this gem of information. I settled myself behind the steering wheel, switched on and felt for the gear lever. There wasn't one! I had never driven an automatic before, nor had any of the others, but somehow we managed to find the Rockefeller complex which we circled, looking for a garage entrance. Fortunately a large white-gloved negro commissionaire appeared, waved us down, remarked 'He's been at the sauce again, I see,' allowed us to alight, pointed us in the correct direction for the Vanderbilt and drove the 'body' away.

The next day we returned to Canada and after a couple of days were sent to Halifax to get a ship back to the U.K. We boarded the vessel, only to be told that we were unexpected and would have to sleep in a double row of hammocks. SNAFU, as our American friends say – Strictly Normal All Fouled(?) Up. The crossing was not very pleasant. Extremely cramped quarters, a tiny beer ration – one queued for a pint and when eventually served, immediately rejoined the queue. Exigencies of the Service, as they say. We also had several submarine alerts, which made us feel great sympathy for the sailing types. We would far rather have been in our aircraft. Much safer, we thought.

Chapter 17

BLIGHTY

On our return to England in 1943 we were posted to various units, ostensibly to have our 'rest' from operational duties. I was sent as a Navigation Instructor to R.A.F. Honeybourne, an O.T.U. (Operational Training Unit) in Warwickshire which had Ansons and the notorious 'flying coffins', the Whitleys. After being given a billet and a bicycle, a basic necessity on such a spread-out unit, I was granted seven days leave. I spent two days with my widowed mother who lived in Hove and then went to Romford in Essex to see my girlfriend Vicky. When I had last heard from her she had been in a 'reserved occupation' with the Ford Motor Company at Dagenham and I was not a little shattered when her mother told me that she had volunteered for the W.A.A.F and was doing her basic training at R.A.F. Innsworth. I proceeded thither at a high rate of knots. Vicky managed to get a thirty-six hour pass, and I booked a double room at a local hostelry. Weren't we naughty!

I returned to RAF Innsworth with Vicky and after some cajoling was able to persuade her postings officer to promise me that if a vacancy should come up at R.A.F. Honeybourne in the Equipment Accounts Section, the trade that Vicky was training for, she would do her best to arrange a posting for Vicky. Flight-Sergeant operational aircrew evidently had some sort of influence with young junior W.A.A.F. officers! After some weeks Vicky duly arrived at Honeybourne, the day after I was posted to its satellite, Long Marston, some six miles away. Exigencies of the service again! Our bicycles did much mileage. On evenings when we were not on duty I would ride half-way to Honeybourne to meet Vicky, we would then both cycle to Stratford-upon-Avon, sink a few jugs of bitter, pedal back to Honeybourne and then I would return to Long Marston, a round trip of about twenty-five miles for me. I must have been fit in those days.

The pupil navigators sent to us were Canadians, and a great number of them were commissioned. It became a little awkward for me as a Senior N.C.O. having occasionally to say, 'That was a stupid bloody error, sir!' and my Flight Commander suggested that I apply for a commission. I pointed that I had been on that so-called mutiny in the Middle East and felt that any such application would be turned down flat. The Flight Commander said that he would recommend me anyway and thought that my 'docs', my service record, would have not arrived in the U.K. yet. So I applied as suggested, passed muster with the C.O. at Long Marston and then had to go before the Station Commander at Honeybourne. He, too, said that I had had strong recommendations and that he would forward my application to Group Headquarters with his O.K. As I was about to leave his office he called me back to say that my 'docs' had arrived from the Middle East, but he was ignoring them.

After a short period I was summoned to Group H.Q. for an interview with the A.O.C. This was it! I was slightly terrified, but I need not have been. The A.O.C. was charm itself. He told me to sit down and relax and said that I had been strongly recommended for a commission and he hoped that I was disciplining those Canadian characters. He agreed with me that Canadians as individuals were first-class fellows, but their discipline seemed to deteriorate when they were en masse. I told him that one toilet wall had the inscription 'F.Sgt. Egles is a bastard' and he told me, 'I'm delighted to hear it.' He then said that my records mentioned the 'mutiny' at R.A.F. Kabrit, and that he had known the Group Captain Station Commander when he was a Flying Officer, 'and he always was a silly sod!' I could not argue with an officer of Air Rank, could I? The A.O.C. then informed me that he had interviewed several of us 'mutineers' in the previous few months and that he had personally recommended all of them. He pointed out that his was not the final say in our case but that the Air Council would have to decide. I returned to my unit feeling rather more hopeful and carried on with my duties. Shortly after that I was due for promotion to Warrant Officer and on applying was told 'Oh, no, you're up for a commission.' So I soldiered on.

I was lucky enough to be sent to R.A.F. Abingdon near Oxford to attend a GEE instructors course. GEE was a navigational and blind-bombing device introduced into R.A.F. service during August 1941. The GEE system consisted of the reception by equipment in the aircraft of transmissions from three ground stations situated on a base line approximately 200 miles (322 km) long. One of these transmitters was known as the 'A' or 'Master' station and the other two were called the 'B' and 'C' or 'Slave' stations. Each 'Slave' transmission was locked to the 'Master' transmission and the difference in the time taken by the 'A' and the 'B' and the 'A' and the 'C' signals to reach the aircraft were measured and displayed on a CRT (Cathode Ray Tube) on the navigator's table in the aircraft. From them the aircraft could be located on two position lines known as the 'GEE co-ordinates', and the ground position of the aircraft coincided with the point at which these co-ordinates, which were printed as a grid on special GEE charts, intersected.

The co-ordinates could be obtained by a competent navigator in less than a minute. The accuracy of a GEE fix varied from less than half a mile to about five miles, depending on the skill of the navigator, upon whether the aircraft was in an area where the GEE grid intersected acutely or obtusely and upon the distance of the aircraft from the transmitters. The range of GEE itself varied with conditions from three to four hundred miles, but in general, the rule was that the greater the range, the less was the accuracy.

The course was so secret that we had to show our Forms 1250 (the R.A.F. Identity Document) each time we entered and *left* the lecture room, and we were not allowed to take notes in any form.

Long Marston was surrounded by farms and I recall three incidents connected with the farm animals which I feel are worth recounting.

The first concerns a Whitley in which I was flying with a pupil navigator on a short night-flying exercise which we had completed satisfactorily, but the landing seemed somewhat bumpier than usual. When we got to de-briefing there was not a little consternation. The Flight-sergeant ground crew wanted to know how the mainplane had got covered in blood and added that the local farmer was rather upset because one of his cows was bellowing with pain with most of the skin missing from its back. The ending to that incident could have been much more serious.

The other two tales involved my billet – the normal wartime hut with a central corridor with rooms on either side. I shared my room with another Flight-sergeant, Smithy, and on this particular night we had been into Stratford-on-Avon on our bikes and partaken of a goodly ration of bitter. At about 01.00 hours I woke to a call of nature. There were toilets, outside, at either end of our hut and I turned left out of our room door to be faced by a very large horse. Thinking that the bitter had been stronger than usual, I smartly about-turned and used the facility at the opposite end of the billet but on returning, the horse was still there. I felt that Smithy needed to be informed, so I woke him to tell him of the corridor's occupant. 'Push off!' - or words to that effect was his first reaction but being wakened caused him to need the loo. Moments later a rather shaken Smithy returned agreeing that there was indeed a horse in the corridor. The last room in the hut was the abode of the Station Warrant Officer and we felt that, as the senior bod in the billet, he should be told of our new tenant. The following conversation took place after we had gingerly woken the S.W.O.

Us: 'Sir, there's a horse in the passage.'

SWO: 'You're drunk, go back to bed!'

Us: 'Seriously, sir, there's a horse in the passage.'

SWO: 'Go away!'

Us: 'Please come and look, sir.'

SWO: 'Oh, O.K.' - then, - 'My God, you're right!'

By this time the other occupants of the billet were awake and between us we were able to usher the poor bewildered animal outside.

Again a story about a different billet. The next room to ours was occupied by two 'store-bashers', Senior N.C.O.s in the Equipment section who were very house-proud. Their floor was always brightly polished, the room left in an immaculate condition and the door left open wide to expose the glory of the accommodation to any passer-by. Our room was rather more homely and the door firmly closed as were all the others in the hut. One day Smithy and I were returning to our quarters after duty and as we neared the door were assailed by the most awful pong. On attempting to enter, we found the passage jammed solid by two cows who were trying to extricate themselves from their unaccustomed surroundings. It appeared that the unfortunate creatures had been in the hut for some considerable time. The floor was inches deep in excreta and their horns had ripped holes in the plaster board walls. One had got her rear end through the door of our house-proud neighbours and had done nothing at all to improve the polish on the floor. We were all 'evacuated' to other quarters and the sanitary squad did its best, but to my knowledge that particular hut was never occupied by human beings again.

At the beginning of April 1943, Vicky and I decided that it would be a good idea to get married. In those days Service personnel could purchase a Special Licence extremely cheaply, which allowed them to get married very quickly without the usual time required for the posting of banns. We each managed to obtain some leave, seven days for Vicky and ten days for myself at the end of the month. I hied myself to Vicky's home at Barking in Essex, (Vicky was to follow me in a couple of days), and her mother accompanied me when I went to give notice of the wedding at the Register Office at Ilford. All went swimmingly until the Registrar said to me 'And is this the prospective bride?' I soon disillusioned him! Vicky arrived on the Wednesday, together with Mac, a navigator colleague of mine, who was to be my best man at the wedding on the Saturday. He was a fellow of great contrasts. In peace time he taught Classics at a Scottish college and he played the hottest jazz trumpet I had ever heard by an amateur. Mac had not been operational, because after qualifying as a navigator he developed a stomach ulcer and was not permitted to fly for trips of more than half an hour. He was also forbidden whisky, which for a Scot must have been purgatory. Every now and then, though, Mac would say, 'Och, ta hell with it' and partake of a few drams. This usually put him in bed for a day but he always said that it was worth it.

Our wedding party was neither large nor lavish. There were Vicky's parents and sister, her friend Jeannette as matron-of honour, my mother, Mac, my best man and of course the bride and groom. All went successfully, and the best man was poured on to the train. My mother stayed with my mother-in-law and Vicky and I spent our honeymoon in my mother's bungalow in Hove. Money was *very* short in those days.

ACW1 Egles and Flight Sergeant Egles returned to their respective units to get on with the war. For my part, life as an instructor began to pall and I applied, without success, to get back on an operational squadron. A great deal of off-duty cycling was done by Flight Sergeant and Mrs. Egles and at the end of May Vicky announced that she was pregnant, which, of course, meant that she would have to leave the WAAF when the pregnancy was of six months duration. Dad-to-be, naturally had to soldier on – if that is the right expression for an airman.

One day when I was on duty in the Nav. Office the phone rang and a voice said, 'May I speak to Pilot Officer Egles, please?' I replied that I was Flight Sergeant Egles and knew of no Pilot Officer Egles. The caller then informed me that he was the A.O.C's P.A. (Personal Assistant) and had been asked by the A.O.C. to contact me and inform me that the 'mutiny' charge had been written off, and that I was now a commissioned officer. I went to the Station Orderly Room, where my good news was confirmed, collected my basic uniform grant and some leave and wended my way to London to get my P.O's uniform. I had already been informed that I would be permitted to stay on the same station, Long Marston.

After spending some days in town getting kitted out as far as the allowance, which I believe was £100, permitted, I returned to

Long Marston and was given a billet in the officers' quarters. As I was unpacking my kit an aged (he must have been over 50!) airman appeared and said that he was George, my batman and would be pleased to 'look after me'. I knew that I had to report to the Station Commander the next day, so I asked George if he could do anything about getting a decent shine on my new buttons. I had tried but had made very little impression – they still looked too new. He assured me that he would do his best and that all his 'gentlemen' were properly turned out. The next morning George appeared with my new best uniform and the buttons had an almost blinding shine. I never did find out how George had performed such an apparent miracle. When I questioned him, all I could get in reply was, 'Ah, sir, tricks of the trade you know. I've been doing this job for many years.'

I duly reported to the C.O. feeling like an advertisement for how the well-dressed R.A.F. officer should look. I felt very proud with my Pilot Officer's 'ring' on my sleeves. The C.O. welcomed me to his office, offered me a chair, congratulated me on receiving my commission and said he would join me in a drink in the Mess that evening. After our little chat ended, I replaced my hat, stood smartly to attention and gave a parade ground salute. As I was opening the office door to leave he called out to me in a rather harsh voice, 'Mr. Egles, the next time you speak to me, will you do me the honour of appearing correctly dressed!' Horrors! What on earth had I done? Were my flies unbuttoned? Were my shoes unlaced? Feeling most embarrassed I mumbled falteringly, 'Please, sir, would you kindly inform me what is wrong?' A beaming smile came over the C.O.'s face, and in a much friendlier tone he said, 'Your rank is incorrect. Your commission took so long to come through that your automatic promotion to Flying Officer has taken effect. Again, congratulations.' I left the interview a very happy man indeed. On looking back, it appears that although I married as a Flight Sergeant, I was by then a Pilot Officer, but of course I didn't know.

One day I was in Flying Control when we heard what was obviously a large aircraft circling overhead. It was a Short Stirling, a four-engined monster which none of us had actually seen before, but of course were able to recognise as we were required to keep up to date with our Aircraft Recognition. The pilot obviously wished to land and the Airfield Control officer gave it a 'green' with an Aldis lamp. The Stirling landed, beautifully, I may say, and taxied round to just outside Flying Control. Most of us dashed outside to get a closer look and watched the front hatch open and a ladder lowered. A rather short figure in full flying kit descended, removed its flying helmet to display shoulder-length golden hair. It was a girl! We waited for the rest of the crew to appear, to no avail. The petite blonde *was* the crew! She explained that she was a member of the Air Transport Auxiliary and had flown most types of aircraft, and could we please supply her with lunch? This, of course, we were pleased to do. After lunch the young lady said that she had half an hour to spare and could she possibly have a game of snooker? Our Mess expert said that he would be delighted to give her a game, but he was not so delighted when she absolutely thrashed him. Having thanked us for entertaining her, the glamorous pilot went back to her aircraft, took off and beat us up as if she were flying a Spitfire. And I didn't even get her name!

Chapter 18

P.F.F. TRAINING

By now some of us were becoming 'browned off' with instructing and wanted to get back on to operations again, but only some were successful with their applications. One day the luck of the Egles manifested itself. I was on my own in the Navigation Office and answered the phone without giving my name, to be greeted with the message, 'Group H.Q. here. Have you two commissioned navigators who would like to go onto Pathfinders?'

'Yes,' I said immediately, 'Flying Officers Egles D.C. and Palmer L.J.'

Palmer L.J. was my very good 'mate' Len, who I knew was as anxious as I was to get to operational again. The next day orders came through posting us to R.A.F. Upwood in Cambridgeshire for Pathfinder training.

Air Vice Marshal Donald Bennett, an Australian in his early thirties, had formed the Pathfinder Force from the most skilled and experienced crews of Bomber Command, which Group Commanders had been asked to release for these new and special duties - to find and mark the targets for the following main bomber stream, by means of new navigational aids, especially illumination flares dropped over the targets, and ground target indicators. P.F.F. greatly improved the efficiency of Bomber Command in the succeeding months and years.

We were told that after our training we were to be posted to a Halifax Squadron in Italy to bring the navigators up to P.F.F. standard, particularly with regard to use of H2S, a form of radar. The tuition at Upwood consisted mainly of a course to instructor standard on H2S, which had been developed by Dr Lovell at the TRE (Telecommunications Research Establishment). It produced a 'map' on a Cathode Ray Display in the aircraft, and could be used for navigation and for 'blind' bombing – a most useful tool!

Our course at R.A.F. Upwood was mostly theory, Pathfinder principles and simulator practice. We were told about target-marking and route-marking methods with various types of incendiary devices. Very weird sounding (to us) names were given. Wanganui, marking with sky markers – coloured flares – Paramatta, the code name for ground marking with long-burning incendiary bombs of various colours and Newhaven, marking using H2S and backing up visually. The names came from the home-towns of the PFF types who had thought up these various methods. Later we were posted to R.A.F. Newmarket for more practical work.

The Mess was a temporary wartime building in the main road of Newmarket and the airfield was where the racecourse now is. We arrived early on the 11th January 1944, one date I do remember, and found that we were detailed to fly a long cross-country trip from the crack of dawn on the 12th in a Lancaster, a four-engined bomber.

Late that afternoon I received a signal informing me that I had become a father and that mother and son were doing well. Yippee! After dinner we started a pub-crawl of Newmarket to wet the baby's head – and our throats. We returned well oiled to the Mess bar intending to carry on the good work, only to find that the Station Duty Officer had ordered the bar to be closed at 2200 hours, in five minutes time! We managed to persuade the bar steward to fill several large jugs with best bitter and take them into the ante-room, which was unoccupied, apart from two moose heads which graced the end wall. A short time later, one of our company tripped over a pouffe. We decided that it should not have been on the floor causing a hazard for unsuspecting aircrew, so we placed it out of harm's way on one of the low metal rafters which adorned this type of building. This, at the time, seemed a very good idea. Why not put the rest of the furniture up there in case anyone else had a collision with it? Whilst we were performing this useful operation someone noticed that the two moose were unshaven in the Mess. Not the standard one would expect. One of our company had a cut-throat razor which was brought into use with the necessary lather, and the two beasts then displayed a more presentable appearance in the Officers Mess. We carried on with our relocation of dangerous furniture but were unable to place the grand piano on a higher plane. So to bed.

The next morning we ate a hasty breakfast and then took off on our long cross-country radar practice and petrol consumption test. All went well until we returned. Waiting at the dispersal was the Station Adjutant who requested that Flying Officer Egles report to the Station Commander immediately. This I did, in some trepidation. The ensuing conversation went something like this.

S.C.: 'Good afternoon, Egles, we have not met before. It has been brought to my notice that you became a father yesterday and celebrated the fact in rather an unusual fashion.'

Me: 'Good afternoon, sir. I regret I have not paid my respects previously, but you were not available yesterday afternoon.'

S.C.: 'Let us not worry about that, now. Will you and your

friends kindly go at once to the Mess and put the furniture in the ante-room back in proper order. The Mess staff are terrified to touch it.'

Me: 'Yes, sir. Immediately, sir.'

S.C.: 'You may go now. Congratulations on your parenthood. By the way, I'm not fond of the moose, either, but please clean the soap off them.'

My great sighs of relief can well be imagined.

When we got back to the Mess we could hardly believe what we had done. It was only with much bribing with promises of many libations that we were able to persuade several bods to help us get the ante-room furniture back on to the floor.

Chapter 19

ITALY

After we had finished our training at Newmarket we were sent to R.A.F. Hurn near Bournemouth to collect a new modified Halifax four-engined bomber aircraft to fly out to Celone near Foggia in Italy to join 462 Squadron in February 1944. The only defensive armament this model of Halifaxes had was a rear turret equipped with four .303 Browning machine guns, but it was fitted with H2S

Our route took us via Maison Blanche, Algiers and Catania in Sicily. On landing at Maison Blanche in Algeria we were greeted over the TR9 (radio) by a deep-brown American voice with the following message: 'If the British four-fan destruction ship will follow the Jeep with the yellow flag we will re-fill you with gas.' So much for the aircraft recognition abilities of our gallant allies.

On the way from Catania to Celone we flew fairly close to Vesuvius, the volcano near Naples, which was in a state of eruption, with a large cloud of smoke covering a considerable area of sky. We flew through the edge of this 'smoke' to discover to our horror that our windscreens had become almost opaque – the volcanic grit in the cloud had scratched the perspex – and it was with great difficulty and skill that the pilot was able to land at our new base.

The runway was made of metal grids laid on the bare earth and our accommodation was in tents. All very basic! We soon settled in and Len and I commenced instructing the crews on the use of the H2S and the Pathfinder route – and target-marking techniques. We also carried out normal operational flying. The rest of my new crew were all senior NCOs, so I didn't see as much of them off duty as I would have liked. We discovered that there were two American heavy bomber squadrons on the same base. They, of course, had wooden floors to their tents, duckboard footpaths, and HOT showers! The weather was not at all 'Sunny Italy'. It was wet, cold and very muddy. Most of our tents were fitted with an ingenious and highly illegal petrol drip-feed heating system constructed by the ever-adaptable mechanical types. It was crude, but did help to make life a little more bearable. There were a few occasions when high winds caused minor conflagrations, but on the whole the advantages outweighed the disadvantages.

The Officers Mess was a marquee which was equipped with a magnificent bar built by the unit 'chippies' (carpenters) and decorated mainly by odd pieces of German aircraft complete with swastikas, collected from crashed enemy planes, and by excellent copies of the famous Varga girls produced by various amateur artists. The only thing missing was a foot-rail at the bar. Someone had noticed that at the unused swimming-bath in Foggia town there was a fine hand rail. It was felt that it was wasted on a defunct swimming-pool, and a small group of us unofficially borrowed an M.T. vehicle and some hacksaws and proceeded Foggia-wards. One of the chaps spoke pretty good Italian and he was detailed to engage the swimming-pool caretaker in conversation and ply him with cigarettes while the rest of us carefully removed a section of the hand-rail which became the foot-rail of the 462 Squadron Officers Mess.

At about the time that the training to P.F.F. standard was complete, the powers that be decided to change the squadron number from 462 to 614. This caused no little chaos with the postal service and for some time we received mail for the previous 614 bods, but all was eventually sorted out.

Life carried on as a pathfinding and target-marking squadron with attacks on such places as Genoa, Sofia, Plovdiv, Budapest and Bucharest when weather conditions permitted. We did not have a 'hard' runway, and the metal strips (P.S.P. Pierced Steel Planking) laid down often buckled on the very soft terrain when heavy aircraft such as our Halifaxes and the U.S.A.A.F. Liberators (I suppose I should call them B.24s) and Flying Fortresses (B.17s) landed on them.

The Americans bombed by day and we bombed by night, and there was some liaison between us. We often attacked the same targets and their Navigation leaders were frequent visitors to our Navigation section. I well remember one such visit when an R.A.F. Mosquito landed. The Americans had never seen one before and the conversation that followed went something like this:

Them: 'Gee, what's that?'

Us: 'A Mosquito - a wooden aeroplane.'

Them: 'What's a little plane like that for?'

Us: 'Oh, P.R. (Photographic reconnaissance) and it's a bomber.'

Them: 'A bomber! Whatever sort of bomb load can a tiny thing like that carry?'

Us: 'Some carry a 4000 lb cookie.'

Them: 'Wow!' and then silence.

Sometimes the famed and massive Flying Fortress carried only 4000 lbs of bombs. One up for the R.A.F.

Chapter 20

BUDAPEST

A certain navigator, who shall be nameless, was Joint Squadron Navigation Officer, and had briefed the Squadron on the route to be taken to Budapest from their base at Foggia in Italy, for a bombing op. on which he was also to fly. After take-off, the aircraft was to climb to 10,000 ft. over base and then set course on a bearing which had been given before take-off.

At about 5,000 ft., the navigator unpacked his navigation bag, and was horrified to find that he had picked up the spare bag from the Navigation Office, and not the one containing his meticulously prepared charts for the op. - no maps! All that was available to him was a blank Mercator H2S chart, which did not extend northwards as far as the target, the marshalling yards at Budapest. Fortunately, the latitude and longitude of Budapest were firmly fixed in the mind of the, by now, thoroughly ashamed navigator, and he was able to construct a Mercator graticule on his navigation table, carry on navigation, mostly with the aid of the H2S, and successfully mark the target.

The rest of the crew were not told of his misdemeanour until after the return to base. It was the usual practice for navigators to hand in their charts as well as logs of the op. to the Squadron Navigation Officer on return from an op. In this case our careless navigator had to bribe the 'Chiefy' Ground Crew to unbolt the navigation table and have it taken to his fellow Squadron Navigation Officer for checking.

This escapade resulted in a large increase in the sinner's (my) wine bill.

Chapter 21

P.O.W.

On the 7th May 1944 my crew were detailed to mark and attack the marshalling yards at Bucharest from our base at Foggia on the heel of Italy. In the afternoon we had a visit from our American friends who had bombed Romania that morning, to tell us that the weather was wonderful, without a cloud in the sky. We did not want that sort of weather; we wanted some cloud cover as there was a full moon. In cloud we could navigate and mark the target with our radar. We pointed out the Yanks' weather information to our Met. Officer who assured us that as soon as the sun went down the cloud would build up as we crossed the Yugoslavian mountains and give us all the cover we required.

We duly took off, climbed on track over the Adriatic and the Yugoslavian mountains but there was not a cloud in sight. Of course we pressed on, marked a route point for the bombers following us and marked and bombed our target, the Bucharest marshalling yards. So far so good. We had turned on to our homeward course and were proceeding merrily westward when Paddy, the rear-gunner shook us all by calling over the intercom, 'Bandit to port – corkscrew – NOW!'

We were at 20,000 feet in bright moonlight and with a cloudless sky it seemed almost like daylight. Norrie the pilot flung the Halifax about as if it was a Tiger Moth but to no avail. A rocket from the attacking Ju.88 came through the fuselage into the mainplane which immediately caught on fire and started to buckle. A Halifax will not fly with only one wing so the skipper ordered us to bale out. Remembering how cold it had been on my previous experience behind enemy lines I decided to keep my flying helmet on and carefully tucked the intercom cable into my battle blouse before leaping into the night. We had heard tales of some aircrew being shot at whilst descending by parachute so I did a delayed drop - counting about forty before pulling the ripcord. On my doing so the chute harness shot up above me and caught the right hand earphone of my helmet, tearing my ear slightly. Below me I could see the Danube shining in the moonlight. I could not tell whether I was going to land in it, south of it in Bulgaria or north of it in Romania. The wind decided my destination - Romania. On reaching terra firma, I bent my legs and rolled over in the prescribed fashion, finding myself in a soft muddy field, only to bang my left ear on the only rock for umpteen square miles around. I now had blood coming in quite large quantities from both ears. Not very painful but rather messy!

My first job was to hide my parachute, which I did beneath some convenient bushes, and then I started walking westwards - towards Yugoslavia. Stars were still visible, including Ursa Major so I was able to check my direction. I walked for about a couple of hours before I saw any signs of habitation, some buildings of what appeared to be a farm. I carefully circumnavigated these and after a short while decided to rest in the remains of a haystack. The next thing I remember was waking up surrounded by dogs barking and peasants waving pitchforks. I tried to explain who I was, to no avail, and they 'escorted' me back to the farmhouse. There the farmer himself spoke to me and I discovered that he had some knowledge of French, as I had. They had all, at first, thought I was German as the Luftwaffe uniform was a not totally dissimilar colour to my R.A.F. blue battledress. I pointed out that I was a British officer and the farmer said that he would have to take me into the local village. He gave me some bread and *apa dolce*, literally sweet water, and then drove me in a very dilapidated old truck to the village where he handed me over to the gendarmerie. I was of great interest to the local populace – the first R.A.F. officer they had ever seen. I was 'introduced' to the mayor and his daughter – she also spoke French and asked me if there was anything I needed. I asked for some soap to wash with. She went away and returned with a tiny sliver. It was only much later that I realised what a sacrifice this had been on the part of the young lady.

I spent the night in the local lock-up and was collected by an army truck the next day, together with other members of my crew and some U.S.A.A.F. aircrew, a few of whom were splinted and bandaged. I was naturally delighted that all my crew were safe and well. Paddy the rear-gunner was somewhat disgruntled, rather bruised and had only one flying boot. The drill for a rear-gunner when baling out is to rotate his turret, jettison the doors and bale out backwards at the same time that the pilot leaves. Paddy had followed the correct drill, which must have been very difficult with the Halifax spinning due to the lack of one wing.

He found one foot caught and had to climb up his leg to undo the zip of his flying boot in order to release himself, leaving his boot attached to the aircraft. Not long after reaching the ground he was picked up by a Romanian army patrol who laughed at his lack of footwear. Paddy was well known for being willing to fight anything on two feet and as he was a little upset he waded into the jeering soldiery. They of course responded with rifle butts.

We were told that we were being taken to Bucharest and would then be sent to prison camp. We had almost as many Romanian guards as prisoners on the truck and I asked the officer in charge (who also spoke French as did many educated Romanians, I was to discover later) why there were so many. Did he think that a few unarmed and in some cases, injured prisoners would overcome his men? He replied that the soldiers were to guard us against the people, who had suffered from the bombing. On the journey we stopped at an army camp and I was wheeled into the presence of a Romanian general. It appeared that I was the first R.A.F. officer shot down over Romania. He, of course spoke French and wanted to know why we had killed so many civilians with our bombing. I tried to explain that in war it was almost inevitable that there would be civilian casualties and pointed out that many English civilians had suffered bombing. Then my schoolboy French let me down. I wanted to tell him that as he was a fighting man he should understand this and I said, '*Vous êtes un soldat.*' He then went almost blue in the face and shouted, '*Je ne suis pas un soldat! Je suis un officier! Je suis un général!*' and had me wheeled out. So much for the Egles attempt at diplomacy!

We were taken to the Central Police Station in Bucharest where we were told to take a shower. This of course was to enable them to search our uniforms. They found the small hacksaw blade that was in the hem of my battledress blouse but did not find the magnetised compass hidden beneath my flying brevet. We were then interrogated individually by apparent Gestapo types who threatened all sorts of dire consequences if we did not tell them our Squadron, aircraft type, base aerodrome, number of operations flown, names of crew etc etc. I only gave my name, rank and number, as required by the Geneva Convention. I was then interrogated by two Luftwaffe officers whose English was as good as mine. When I commented on this they informed me that they had both attended English universities. They were very polite and asked me to fill in a long questionnaire, which I declined to do. They then said that for me the war was over and dismissed me.

We prisoners were then paraded and marched through the city to our prison camp, which turned out to be a disused High School with all its windows covered in barbed wire. We were given beds and minimal bedding and a day later the NCOs were separated from the Officer prisoners, the NCOs being sent to the Mihai Viteazui Barracks, which meant that I was separated from my crew, who were all sergeants. Just before he left, Paddy, the rear gunner, who was a sort of human jackdaw, presented me with a hammer, a chisel and several keys which he had found and assumed would be of use. I naturally accepted all with gratitude. I was SBO (Senior British Officer) although I was only a Flying Officer, and I was moved into a room with the senior USAAF officers. There were many more American POWS (about 2,000) than British, (36). The SAO (Senior American Officer) at the time was Major Chester Haas.

The guards were all Romanian, mostly middle-aged and very poorly equipped. Their uniforms were very shoddy and many of their boots were patched *on the uppers.* The Camp Commandant was a short, obese colonel whose knowledge of French was as limited as mine. As none of the POWs spoke Romanian I was made Camp interpreter. There were a couple of German 'ferrets' of course. I got on quite well with the Camp Commandant. I always paid the respect due to his rank and the R.A.F. chaps all kept their beds, bedspaces and themselves tidy. For my sins I was also made Camp Supply Officer and my main duty was issuing toilet paper! The Yanks could not appreciate shortages – the majority of them had only recently left the US – and went

Prisoners of War. R.A.F. Officers Group and prison staff at the Old Schoolhouse, Bucharest, Romania 1944.

D. Egles, left rear, in vest.

through toilet rolls at a rate of knots. I had to introduce a system of rationing. I was also Vice Chairman of the Escape Committee. We did get a few bods out but never away. I once managed to leave, myself, when I found a door left open, but was free for only a few hours. I think one of the problems was my rather large Bomber Command type moustache. The only Romanians who sported such hirsute appendages were at least middle-aged and I was only 23.

We managed to start a tunnel. Some chaps had found a door behind the stage in the old school assembly hall. This door was nailed shut and swathed in barbed wire, which was, of course, an invitation to see where it led. It was opened and was found to give access to a small semi-basement room with a very high window which gave a view of the school yard and was also near the kitchens. It was decided that this would be a good place to start a tunnel in time-honoured POW fashion. The wall was about two feet thick, but with the hammer and chisel bequeathed me by my rear-gunner and various odd bits of metal that had been collected a start was made. All went quite well until metal reinforcing rods were encountered. Each time these were attacked the whole building seemed to reverberate. This problem was overcome in a rather roundabout method. Some chaps volunteered to help in the kitchens, pleading boredom, and by careful timing after meals and with a very complex signalling system they managed to cause a loud clatter of pans at the same moments that the reinforcing rods were being attended to. Once were were through the wall some progress was made. Debris from the tunnel was carefully stowed beneath the stage and the tunnel was 'propped up' with odd pieces of wood taken mainly from beds.

The tunnel was never finished. At one stage water poured in and it was eventually found that we had dug into the water trough of the pig sty which was in the school yard.

Life in the 'camp' was not too pleasant, but bearable. Food was very basic indeed, but none of us starved. A typical menu would be:

Breakfast – Bread and jam and apa dolce (water with sugar in it).

Lunch – Potato soup and beans, with water to drink.

Dinner – Vegetable salad, white cheese, onions and water.

We occasionally had meat stew. The meat was often impossible to define as to its origin. Someone suggested that the Romanians found a beast of some sort and threw a hand grenade at it. A few times animal eyes were found – not very appetising. The cooking and serving was done by Russian prisoners, the 'serving' being the dumping of a large bowl of the food on each table.

One small incident sticks in my mind. We, in the senior officers' room, managed to bribe one of the guards to bring in a bottle of alcohol. It was some form of Slivovitz, apparently made in a bathtub! The bottle was passed round and we each took a mouthful. It really was a powerful potion, so much so that one of the imbibers spat most of his mouthful out onto the floor. The next morning there was a bare patch on the varnished floor, but somehow our stomachs survived.

We had several air raid warnings and several air raids in daylight by the Americans, of course, and at night by the R.A.F. Our 'air raid shelter' was the dining room, a semi-basement, which was better than nothing I suppose. One night the camp seemed to be surrounded by red flares – target markers which must have been dropped by my Pathfinder Squadron. The Schoolhouse was quite near to the marshalling yards which appeared to be the target and as reds usually signified the place to bomb it was rather worrying. A few bombs did drop fairly close to us, but caused no significant problem.

Overcoming boredom was our greatest problem. There were a few books available, including a Bible, which I read right through during my imprisonment, skipping the long lists of who begat whom! The odd pack of playing cards also appeared. I managed to keep reasonably occupied with my duties as S.B.O. and interpreter, giving navigation lessons to various Yank navigators who were very interested in R.A.F. nav. methods, rehearsing for the Camp Concert which we gave, writing odd articles for the Camp news-sheet and taking my shift at tunnelling.

Each month I had to sign for the cigarette ration for the non-U.S.A.A.F. chaps and at the foot of the list of officers there were two names on their own who were not at the camp. When I asked who these two officers were I was told that they were being 'looked after in another place'. Eventually these two types named Marcus and Rubens turned up in R.A.F. uniforms. They were most unforthcoming at first and their English was not perfect. After much questioning over several days – they would only talk to me in the middle of the exercise yard – I found that they were Romanian Jews who had been dropped by the R.A.F. in an attempt to organise a Romanian 'underground'. They had brought several thousand pounds worth of gold sovereigns with them but on landing Rubens had broken a leg and they were soon caught after successfully burying their gold. Somehow their captors had not found the few sovereigns hidden in the heels of their flying boots – they gave me three! Apparently they had received very severe 'interrogation', solitary confinement, salt food and very little water and various other unpleasantnesses, but they had not 'broken'.

One day British Red Cross parcels arrived. The cigarettes and chocolate had all been looted but there was tea. I approached the Camp Commandant and told him that we British would like to invite him to partake of tea with us but unfortunately we did not have a teapot. Could I have permission as Camp Supplies Officer to go into town and attempt to purchase one, as well as various other things like needles and cotton that were needed? It was agreed that if I gave my parole I could make the trip accompanied by his Supplies Officer. The trip was duly arranged. The Romanian Supplies Officer turned out to be a chap who could only speak his own language, so our conversation was nil. All was sign language. We were accompanied by an armed private soldier, but he had to march at least ten yards behind us. There was no democracy in the Romanian army.

I had been told by Marcus which area of the city to make for which he said still had Jewish occupants. When I found a likely-looking store my escort merely waved me in and stayed outside. I had been told by Marcus to use his name - he said it would prove beneficial. I tried this and found that the proprietor spoke French and some English. I explained that what I really wanted was a radio and that I had some gold - the sovereigns. One was changed for me at a very high rate of exchange indeed and I was told that they could get me radio parts, but not immediately. A teapot would also be procured. I did not want to take one back then as I wished to 'go shopping' again, nor did I know whether I would be searched on my return to the School, but I did take back some sewing needles and thread and buttons. On our return to durance vile I was not searched so again I asked the Camp Commandant for permission to try to purchase the teapot. Permission was given to make another trip three days later, which suited me fine.

This time I was able to bring back various radio parts *and* some toilet paper (I was not searched), and I could promise the Colonel that a teapot would be available in a couple of days. I was again allowed the journey out and returned without a teapot but with further radio bits, (still no searches), and some of the experts among the Yanks were able to assemble a working radio receiver. We were thus able to tune in to the local news broadcasts which were translated for us by Marcus and Rubens. By this means we learned that the Russian forces were rapidly approaching Romania, much to our joy. I was allowed out of camp once more and this time I returned with a teapot but the proposed tea party with the Romanian Colonel never did take place. I had, however, made arrangements to collect some 'civvies' if I were able to escape again.

This I managed to do a few days later. By now, the Russians were very close to the city and the Germans were leaving, not without bombing the place. During my stay in Bucharest I was bombed by the USAAF by day, the R.A.F. by night, the Red Air Force by day and the Luftwaffe for three days of continuous terror.

Security at the camp was more relaxed, perhaps because of the imminent arrival of the Russians. On this exit from captivity I sacrificed my rather large moustache, of which I was very proud. As I explained earlier, decent sized moustaches were only worn by middle-aged or elderly Romanians. I returned to my friendly shopkeeper who, true to his word, had some civilian clothes for me. They were not of Savile Row quality nor did they fit particularly well, but one does not look a gift suit in the mouth. I met a Romanian architect, who gave me accommodation and fed me. He spoke French and some Russian.

My original plan had been to get to Constanta on the Romanian coast of the Black Sea and somehow move on down to Turkey. The arrival of the Russian army altered my plans. I foolishly assumed that the Russians would help me. We approached a Russian captain who was standing in a side street with a Jeep. The architect told the Russian that I was a British officer and he laughed and said the British were all 'armchair soldiers'. Since I had been shot down twice on my *first* tour, I felt a little upset. I said that I was pleased to see that he was using an American vehicle, but he insisted that it had been made in Russia. The fact that 'Willy's Detroit' was stamped on the back panel in large letters did not impress him at all. It soon became obvious that I could expect no help from the Red Army. The next day I heard that the Americans were sending aircraft to collect their POWs so I headed back to camp.

US Colonel James A. Gunn, the then Senior Allied Officer at the POW camp, had approached the Romanian Foreign Minister, V.C. Georgescu to ask his help in evacuating the ex-POWs, who had been released by then. He introduced Gunn to a Romanian Air Force Officer, Captain Carl Cantacuzino, a 35-year-old descendant of the Romanian royal family and a former stunt pilot. Cantacuzino had had an English governess and had been educated in England, so he was decidedly pro-British, although he had flown with the Luftwaffe. Gunn persuaded Cantacuzino to fly him to Bari in Italy. The first plan was to use an old Isotta Fraschini, which would never have reached Bari. They eventually flew in a Messerschmitt 109 stripped down as far as possible, with American Stars and Stripes painted on each side. Gunn was screwed down inside the fuselage, lying prone in the radio compartment. With them they took their plans for the evacuation of the Allied aircrews. They flew without oxygen at 21,000 ft, not a very pleasant experience!

Once in Bari they left the plane, Cantacuzino in his blue and gold Romanian uniform, and Col. Gunn was able to organise umpteen Flying Fortresses with their fighter escort to fly to Bucharest to pick up the POWs, (including me), in all well over a thousand American and British POWs. Cantacuzino led the way back to Bucharest in a new Mustang aircraft, which he had never flown until that day.

The take-off of these planes from the Poptesti-Leordeni airfield happened to coincide with the entry of the Russian troops on to the Otopeni-Baneasa airfield on the other side of Bucharest. There was great anxiety as to whether the rescue could be carried out on one side of the town whilst the Russians were coming in on the other. In the event, all passed off successfully.

We arrived back at Bari to a great reception of brass band, film cameras etc. but *not* for the non-Americans. No-one seemed to want to know us. I eventually found a British Army Major who was apparently British liaison, but he was most unhelpful. It would seem that he had never previously been required to deal with ex-POWs so had no idea what to do with us. He did manage to find us a billet, and provide some food, but when asked for clothing, he said he had no authority to issue clothing.

I was completely fed up and walked into the town to see what I, as S.B.O. of our POW camp, could do. The only place I knew in Bari was the Albergo Imperiale, which was the Officers Club, and I made straight for it. I must have been a pretty sorry sight. I was wearing rather tatty civilian clothes and had about three days beard, but I was very cross and marched straight into the Club, past various commissioned types of all services and made my way directly to the bar. I banged on the counter and called for a large scotch. Of course I had no Italian money, but I did not care. Then the luck of the Egles came to the fore again. A voice from the other end of the bar called out, 'I suppose you expect me to pay for that!' It was my old friend and colleague, Len Palmer, on a short leave from our Squadron. I told him of my predicament regarding the other POWs and the lack of help from the Brits at the aerodrome.

While we were talking, lo and behold, there appeared a civilian who had arrived in Bucharest very recently. He was apparently a *Times* correspondent and he said that he knew a few of the powers that be at Bari and he would see what he could do. Len, fortunately, had a spare uniform which he would lend me, and as we were of the same rank, trade, height and build, after a shave and a bath I was able to make myself presentable. We returned to the bar to find the *Times* chappy, who said rather enigmatically, 'Go back and have another word with the Major.' This I did. What a difference from our previous meeting! He really tried to be helpful. Spare uniforms miraculously appeared and small amounts of cash were advanced. He even offered to lend me his personal shaving kit. Someone must have really shaken him up. I then put my next problem to him. Would he arrange transport for us to rejoin our units? His face really fell at this. 'Oh dear,' he said. 'We definitely have no spare transport. I don't know what to suggest.'

'Thank you very much!' I replied and started walking back into town after telling the rest of my party what the position was.

I had not gone far when I met an American Flight Officer - equivalent to an R.A.F. Warrant Officer - who had been in the Schoolhouse as a prisoner with me. 'Hey, good to see you back in uniform again!' I felt too ashamed to tell him what had happened to us but did say that I was having trouble getting transport back to my Squadron at Foggia. 'Let's see what we can do,' he said, and led me into a nearby American transport depot. 'Fix this officer up with a Jeep, will ya,' he cried, and in a few minutes I was given a Jeep, for which I signed, and was told to hand it back to any American unit when I had finished with it. I was thus able to rejoin my Squadron. My crew had volunteered to stay behind in Bucharest to look after wounded American prisoners until they could be evacuated, so I made my way back to Foggia on my own, courtesy of the American

Forces. The Major back at the airport said that he hoped he would be able to arrange some transport for the rest of the bods in a day or so.

Once back at my base I was able to get a new battledress of my own and to ask the Adjutant to make arrangements for me to get back to England, having been told that I would not be doing any more operational flying. He also applied for membership of the Caterpillar Club for me, membership of which is restricted to those who have saved their lives by the use of a parachute. This was the third club of which I unwillingly became a member. It was also the cause of my joining the fourth of those clubs, the Ex-POW Association. The last club which I became entitled to join was the R.A.F. Escaping Society, for those who have either escaped from a POW camp and made a 'home run', or having been shot down, have 'evaded', i.e., have avoided capture and made it back to base.

I qualify on both these counts, having evaded on the walk back through the North African desert as well as escaping from the POW camp in Romania.

My journey back home to the UK was through various 'lifts' in different aircraft via Catania and Casablanca.

Chapter 22

FLYING TRAINING COMMAND

On arrival back in Blighty I was told that I was now a Flight Lieutenant, given ten days leave where I was able to collect the rest of my belongings which had been sent home to my wife, Vicky, and told to report to R.A.F. Brackla at the end of it.

R.A.F. Brackla was an Aircrew Allocation Centre near Nairn on the north-east coast of Scotland. I duly arrived at the railway station at Nairn, rang the Transport Section at Brackla and asked for transport to the camp.

I was transferred to a voice that said, 'Duty driver here.'

I replied, 'This is Flight Lieutenant Egles, may I please be picked up from Nairn station?'

'Right-ho, old boy, be about half-an-hour.'

I thought that it was rather too familiar a reply, but was somewhat taken aback when my transport arrived driven by a Squadron Leader pilot. He explained that the lowest form of life at Brackla was Sergeant and anyone could be asked to do any job on the Unit. On our way into the camp we passed a fairly large area of concrete which had charred pieces of timber upon it. 'That, old boy, was the Sergeants Mess. They had a bit of a party there last week. It seems it got a bit out of hand.'

I was billeted in a Nissen hut with several other officers and found out that everyone in it had completed at least one tour of operations and was awaiting 'Allocation'. The hut was heated by one of the old-fashioned circular stoves, which although a bit primitive did give out a satisfactory amount of heat provided they were kept well filled and stoked. There were no such things as batmen at Brackla, so everyone took turns to be Duty Stoker. Over the next few days we were given various written and practical 'tests' to complete. I always have enjoyed I.Q. type puzzles and problems.

There was little to do in the evenings, but there was a bus into Nairn, where there was a cinema. Somebody found out that a film was showing which we particularly wanted to see, so a few of us took the bus to Nairn, only to find that the performance was not due to start for an hour, so to while away the time we found a pub near the cinema to quench our thirsts. The local brew was very much to our liking, and somehow we missed the film. The next evening we made our way to Nairn once more, determined to visit the cinema but it was pouring with rain so we were again forced to spend the hour's wait at the hostelry. Of course, one cannot go into a pub without partaking of a noggin. We never did see the film!

A day or so later I was told to report to the postings officer. He said that I was a confounded nuisance. The 'tests' that we had done were to decide whether we were to get academic or practical postings and I had apparently got very high, but equal, marks in both series of tests. He had therefore decided that I should go to R.A.F. Shawbury to the then Empire Air Navigation School to take the Staff Navigation Course. Unfortunately there were no vacancies at the moment, so would I mind instructing at an Air Navigation School? I didn't mind where I went as long as I could still do some flying. I was posted to R.A.F. Dumfries in Scotland, to await my course at R.A.F. Shawbury, and await it I did.

Just before Christmas Vicky, my wife, announced that she was pregnant again. Great joy! I was the only child of quite aged parents and I had always said that if I got married I would like to have at least two children while I was still young. It looked as if my wishes were being granted. Early in the new year Vicky came up to see me for a few days, leaving Jim, our son, with her mother. Vicky stayed at a pub in Dumfries and some of the chaps on the unit came in with me to have a pint or two with her. Scottish licensing laws decreed that the consumption of alcohol must cease at 21.00 hours, except for bona fide travellers. As a bona fide traveller Vicky was permitted to entertain about twenty of us until about midnight. Laws can often be bent, can't they? In February, Vicky decided that she would like to come up to Scotland so that we could be together. As there were no officers married quarters available at R.A.F. Dumfries my Commanding Officer gave me permission to live out, with Jim still staying with his maternal grandmother. We managed to obtain a reasonable though tiny flat in the town and I was able to get an issue bicycle. It meant a five-mile cycle ride, quite often in the very early hours of the morning, if I was detailed for the 'Meteorological Flight', which usually took off at 06.00 hours. The Met. flight was made in order to see if the weather within a reasonable area was fit for the pupil navigators to do their cross-country exercises, and a staff crew was sent up each day to ascertain this.

Life progressed quite smoothly, if impatiently, awaiting the Staff Nav. course, learning to imbibe 'Little Heavies', a popular strong Scottish ale, usually followed by a whisky chaser, to eat and enjoy indigenous delicacies like haggis and to master the intricacies of the eightsome reel. We formed a small concert party and toured several R.A.F. Stations and I also played the drums in the Station dance band. At last the expected posting to

R.A.F. Shawbury, the Empire Air Navigation School in Shropshire, came at the latter part of May, 1945. Vicky went home to my mother as our expected addition to the family was almost due, and I reported to Shawbury, just before the war in Europe ended.

The course was tough. The first couple of weeks we were lectured on stuff we had long forgotten, the next week or so was fairly current gen and then came new information which started by being quite absorbable but soon began to bounce off the brain unless there was much heavy swotting. We even limited ourselves to one half-pint of bitter per evening and it was during the supping of one of these on June 9th that I received a phone call to tell me that my daughter Vicki had been born and that both she and her mother were doing well. I did partake of a small scotch in celebration, but nothing occurred like the thrash when Jim was born in the previous year. We on the course took a break on each Saturday evening if we were in this country to go into Shrewsbury for a few jugs, often staying overnight and coming back to Shawbury on the Sunday afternoon.

We could suddenly be told to collect an aircraft and go and photograph Rockall, a tiny island in the Atlantic Ocean some two hundred miles west of the Outer Hebrides, or fly to Gibraltar or Reykjavik, the capital of Iceland. By the end of the course we were expected to be able to navigate anything anywhere in the world. When the course was completed we had a rather boozy party and I was given a week's leave and posted to an Air Navigation School at R.A.F. Chipping Warden.

I had not been long at Chipping Warden when I was promoted to Acting Squadron Leader and made Chief Navigation Instructor, which meant less lecturing, but a great deal of administration. Life progressed fairly smoothly and one day we were told that we were moving to R.A.F. Swanton Morley in Norfolk. The C.O. detailed me to be Officer i/c Advance Party, which meant that I had to do the initial take-over at our new unit. He, the C.O., told me to take his car and that he would be flying up with the rest of the unit in about a week's time, so off I went in the issue Hillman Minx with a Flying Officer and a Warrant Officer, having been warned not to use too much fuel but told that we could make a trip into Norwich when our duties were complete. The take-over went satisfactorily. Part of the duty involved inspecting all buildings, and when we checked the bomb dump we found a box containing six silver teapot lids. Not exactly treasure trove, but the Warrant Officer, Wimpy Yeman, (so-called because he had survived two tours in Wellingtons) was one of those types who could turn his hand to anything; he filed off the knobs of the teapot lids and flattened the rims to make very presentable ash trays. We gave one to the C.O., one to the Officers Mess, one to the Sergeants Mess, Wimpy kept one and I received one, which I have to this day, although I gave up smoking over twenty years ago.

On the final Saturday of the take-over we hied ourselves to Norwich in the Minx and supped ales in a pub until almost closing time. By now, Wimpy wanted to know where all the girls were and on enquiring at the bar he was informed that on Saturday night most females were to be found at the 'Muscles'. This was the local name for a venue called the 'Samson and Hercules', where there was dancing. We managed to find the 'Muscles' and parked the car fairly nearby. By the time we got into the dance hall and had had a refreshing draught the place was closing for the night and all the members of the opposite sex appeared to have dancing partners. We wandered back to the car park to discover to our horror that the C.O's vehicle was missing. After some trouble stumbling about in the blackout we managed to find a Police Station. In we went and I told the Sergeant that I wished to report the apparent theft of a car. The following conversation ensued.

Sgt. 'What make of car was it?'

Self. 'Hillman Minx.'

Sgt. 'What colour?'

Self. 'R.A.F. camouflage.'

Sgt. 'What registration number?'

Self. 'I've no idea.'

Sgt. 'Where did you leave it?'

Self. 'I don't really know. In a car park.'

Sgt. 'So, you expect us to find a car of unknown registration number and you don't know where you left it.'

I explained that it was not my personal vehicle but that I would be able to get the registration number for him later, and that if he could produce a map of the city I was fairly sure that I could pinpoint the car park that we had used. This he did, and I showed him the place on the map.

We then had the problem of getting back to Swanton Morley that night. The C.O. was due to arrive by air the next day, and I had visions of having to pay for one Hillman Minx, Commanding Officers for the use of. I asked the Police Sergeant, who by then must have been convinced that I had an extremely low intelligence quotient, if he could suggest how we could get back to base. He obviously took pity on us poor simple airmen and said that he did happen to have a relation who ran a taxi business, and that if he could persuade him to make the journey it would cost us a fiver. This of course was a small fortune in those days but we managed to scrape it together between us and the taxi took us back to Swanton Morley.

The next morning I spent in great trepidation. How would my C.O. take the loss of his personal vehicle? Would I be demoted from Acting Squadron Leader to Aircraftman Second Class? He, the Wing Commander, was due to arrive at lunchtime and I was feeling most apprehensive when I was approached by one of the mess staff at mid-morning who said that he had had a message that an R.A.F. transport had been found abandoned in somebody's garden in the village. 'Go and collect it, whatever it is. It doesn't matter if it is a Queen Mary (a very large R.A.F. vehicle),' I said. Once again the luck of the Egles came to my rescue. The vehicle was the Wing Commander's car. What a good piece of good fortune that the person who had 'borrowed' it should have abandoned it so near its rightful home! I was thus able to meet the C.O. with a clear conscience. I did not tell him the sorry tale until after dinner that evening, and he appeared quite amused by the whole episode. Whew!

Life as a trainer of navigators progressed quite smoothly although we did hear rumours that aircrew training was being phased out. One course was due to be given their brevets in a few days when we were ordered by the powers above that this was not to take place. Having to tell these chaps that all their hard work and study had been to no avail was about the worst thing that I ever had to do.

People by now were being demobilised and I applied for a permanent commission, only to be told that permanent commissions were not being granted, but that I could apply for an extended service commission of four years. This I did, and it was granted.

At about this time a nearby fighter group headquarters was closing down and my C.O. was invited to their farewell party. The Wing Co. asked me to go in his place and when I asked him for transport he told me that the Medical Officer was also going and would be using an ambulance, so I could get a lift from him. The doc. and I duly arrived at the 'little aeroplane' H.Q.

which was a fairly large country house, and were soon in the thick of some fairly hairy drinking. At about 23.00 hours the M.O. had to return to Swanton Morley as he was on duty at midnight and he left me carousing with the fighter types and a few Fleet Air Arm and Army bods. I should mention here that I had regrown my moustache to its full wingspan.

I'm afraid that I do not remember a great deal about the latter hours of the party, but I do remember waking up in the morning recumbent in an armchair. A head poked through a door and informed me that there was still some breakfast left in the dining room, but I would have to hurry. I had to forego a wash, as I was in desperate need of sustenance. I found the dining room and helped myself to cornflakes. When I had eaten them I wiped my moustache with my table napkin, as was my wont, and something seemed strange, but I was not wide awake (or sober?) enough to work out what it was. I finished my breakfast, found the wash-room and was washing my face and looking into the mirror when I discovered what the strange feeling had been. Some miscreant had carefully amputated the port side of my moustache. I searched in vain for someone to lend me some scissors to complete the removal, but could find no one. Then there was the problem of returning to my unit. I found my greatcoat, but not my headgear, and on wandering outside the house found the M.T. (Motor Transport) section in the stables. There were two W.A.A.F.s on duty who on my approach immediately started giggling. I was about to remonstrate with them when I realised that with greatcoat, no hat and half a moustache I must have presented an amusing spectacle.

However I did manage to persuade them to take me to the gate of my unit, as it was only a slight diversion from their proposed journey to Norwich. On my passing through the gate the sentry looked rather hard at me, then recognised me and saluted with a smile. I warned him not to laugh and proceeded to the Officers Mess and called into the Mess Secretary's office to be greeted with 'My God, what's happened to you?'

'Just organise me a large scotch will you, please?' I replied, which he did. I was just partaking of this much needed hair of the dog when the door opened and in came the C.O. He, too, was suitably amused, and instructed me not to shave off the starboard side of my face fungus until the rest of the Mess had seen how I had been treated by the Fighter types. I had, of course, to obey orders and was treated to many sympathetic noggins that evening. The next morning I was able to tidy my face up and start to grow the appendage again.

Chapter 23

CIVVY STREET

By now, I had started to consider my future. Although I had accepted a Short Service Commission I began to worry what would happen to me if I was not able to obtain a Permanent Commission at the end of the four years. I now had the responsibility of a wife and two children and no civilian qualifications. All I really knew about was air navigation, and the civilian airlines only wanted pilots and pilot-navigators, and I assumed that any retraining schemes would be unavailable by then.

My decision was then to leave the R.A.F., get some suitable civilian qualifications and then rejoin. To cut a long story short, I qualified as a teacher and then I re-applied to return to the R.A.F. in 1948.

The interviewing boards were no problem and I was told that as I was getting rather long in the tooth – I was then at the ripe old age of 27 – I would not be expected to fly in jet aircraft, and was informed that I could return as a Flight Lieutenant, dependant on my passing the medical board the next day. This held few fears for me as I felt very fit, although I was slightly worried as to whether I would be able to blow the mercury column up for the necessary length of time. My fears on this point proved groundless, but I was rather concerned when it came to the hearing tests. No longer did the examining medical officer whisper across the room and ask one to repeat what he said. Now one was shut in a sound-proof box with earphones and tested with a variety of electronic noises.

At the end of all the tests I was summoned before the president of the board to be greeted with, 'Egles, I'm afraid you're unfit to fly jets. You are high tone deaf in your right ear.' I replied that I was not going to be flying jets, only to be told, 'An aircrew officer in the Royal Air Force must be fit to fly anything, anytime, anywhere. I'm sorry.'

I was, of course, very upset about this and the next day I approached the Air Ministry to ascertain if there were any other jobs I could do. After another interview I was offered a commission in the Equipment Branch with the rank of Flying Officer. This I turned down as I really wanted to fly, and so I stuck to teaching. During my career, I spent five years in Uganda as a Headmaster of a school in Kitgum in the North of Uganda and Head of Mathematics department in a college in Jinja. This was in the time of Idi Amin, and there are another chapter or three I could write on my experiences at that time, including a week in gaol, but that does not belong in this book. My wife Vicky died in 1978, and I met and married Eileen, with whom I settled in Bognor Regis. Eventually I became very deaf – 'bilateral sensori – neural deafness, noise-induced, 90% loss, attributable to flying', as the medical board assessed me – and I had to retire early from teaching.

Thus ended my most enjoyable and somewhat eventful career as one of the 'Many'. For those not conversant with the expression, I would have to quote the words of the Prime Minister, Winston Churchill, after the Battle of Britain, when the Fighter aircrew performed so many valiant deeds in the skies over Britain:

'Never in the field of human conflict was so much owed by so many to so few.'

The Press of the time began to call the Fighter crews 'The Few', and the sobriquet has stuck. In recent years, since it has become common knowledge that Bomber Command lost, for example, as many aircrew in *one* raid on Nuremberg as Fighter Command lost in the whole of the Battle of Britain, Bomber aircrew have been called 'The Many', of whom I was just one of the lucky ones.

Dudley and Eileen Egles, 1995

POSTSCRIPT

'There are no words with which I can do justice to the aircrews who fought under my command. There is no parallel in warfare to such courage and determination in the face of danger over so prolonged a period, of danger which at times was so great that scarcely one man in three could expect to survive his tour of thirty operations.'

Marshal of the Royal Air Force Sir Arthur Harris,
C-in-C, Bomber Command.

Truly I was one of the lucky ones, surviving two tours. Since my retirement, I have become actively involved in many clubs and associations connected with the Royal Air Forces. Eileen and I have attended reunions of 148 and 614 Squadrons, the Aircrew Association, the Goldfish Club, the Royal Air Forces Escaping Society, and through our local Royal Air Forces Association Club we do our little bit for the R.A.F. Benevolent Fund. I have also become President of the East Hampshire Branch of the Italy Star Association.

I have met Len Palmer, Peter Mayhew and Norrie Dear again and in 1993 at a reunion at R.A.F. Marham of 148 Squadron, seven of us 'Mutineers' met again, along with our Squadron Commander at the time of the 'mutiny', 'Turkey' Rainsford.

One of the 'Mutineers', Howard Hewer, who was at this reunion, had sent me copies of photographs he had taken immediately on our return from 300 miles behind enemy lines in the North African desert, before we had had time to wash, shave or change our clothes. It was good to talk with him and the others again after fifty years. The 148 Squadron reunion takes place annually.

I am in contact with a number of the U.S.A.A.F. POWs in America, one of whom, Lieut. Col. W.R. 'Dick' Cubbins, invited us in 1987 to his lovely home in Natural Bridge, Virginia to spend two weeks with him and his wife, Lucille. With them we attended a Reunion of the US Ex-POWs Association, where I met again many of those who were in the old schoolhouse with me. I also met there again a remarkable lady, Princess Catherine Caradja of Romania, who, with her daughter, Princess Alexandra Caradja, had been very good to us POWs while we were imprisoned. I kept in contact with Princess Catherine, and Eileen and I attended the sumptuous wedding in Paris of her granddaughter, Hélène-Brianna, Princess Alexandra's daughter. We brought Princess Catherine back after the wedding to spend a week with us, and visited her from time to time until her death at the age of 100 a few years later. She had returned to Bucharest for the last years of her life, and is buried in the grounds of the orphanage her mother founded there. We still visit Princess Alexandra in her Paris home every two years.

Eileen wrote a poetic tribute to us R.A.F. types, which she read out at the US Ex-POW Reunion we attended, and it is with this, perhaps, that I should close this light-hearted account of my service career.

FIFTY YEARS ON
by
EILEEN EGLES

Dashing young heroes, tall, slim and fair,
   Quick-witted, moustached, with luxuriant hair.
A pretty girl passing them brightened their eyes,
   And for freedom they fought in the perilous skies.

O! What has become of those gallant young men,
   Grounded for fifty-odd years since then?
Where are the happy young heroes of old,
   Those Air Force boys of whom legends are told?

     Ah me! ask me not! 'Tis sad to relate
     How those handsome young lads
     Have been treated by fate.
Slim bodies have put on a fair bit of weight;
   Moustaches have drooped, and the hair that of late
Was thick, dark and lustrous is almost not there,
   Just a few thinning strands of fast-greying hair.

That rapier-like wit of long years ago
   Has become so pedestrian, limping and slow;
But one spark remains of those long-ago men,
   One memory stirs them now, as it did then.

When a pretty girl smiles at them, ah – what a sight!
   Backs straighten, heads swivel, eyes smartly right,
For a glimpse of her figure, the tilt of her head;
   Those boys of the old days will never be dead!